Scuba Northeast

By

Robert G. Bachand

Sea Sports Publications
Box 647, Belden Station
Norwalk, CT 06852

Reprinted, 1987

ISBN 0-9616399-0-3

Library of Congress 86-060246

PRINTED IN THE UNITED STATES OF AMERICA

DEDICATION

To my wife and lifelong dive buddy, Kathy
and
to my more recent dive buddies, Rob and Michelle.

Acknowledgements

Many divers, dive shop owners and trawl fishermen shared their valuable information with me. I would , however, like in particular to thank Richard Taracka, Bruce Mackin, Lada Simek, Noel Voroba and my wife, Kathy, for their help and encouragement in the preparation of Volume II.

All fish illustrations by Muriel Sargent

TABLE OF CONTENTS

About the author vi
Foreword vii

Part I
Northeast Diving 1
Tides 2
Depths 3
Currents 3
Visibility 4
Water Temperatures 5
Bringing Home the Bacon 6
Permits 8
Dangerous Marine Animals 8
Common Area Marine Fish 14
Finding a Wreck 20
Underwater Photography 22

Part II
Long Island Sound 34
Fishers Island Sound 76
Coastal Rhode Island 81
Block Island Sound 94
Offshore Wrecks 103
South Shore of Long Island 108
Coastal New Jersey 117

Part III
Inboard Profiles of the USS Bass and San Diego 123
Appendix 131
Suggested Reading 141
Index 145
Diving Accidents DAN, Safety Afloat 151

The Author

Bob, whose avocation is anything to do with the sea, is a pedodontist (children's dentist) in Norwalk, Connecticut. A member of the International Oceanographic Foundation, the American Littoral Society, Oceanic Society (Trustee, 1984-) and the Long Island Sound Taskforce (President 1984-), he has written numerous articles on such diverse subjects as dentistry, photography, marine history and marine biology. His articles have appeared in Skin Diver, Sea Frontiers, Undersea Journal, Underwater Naturalist, Connecticut Magazine. He is co-editor of the Long Island Sound Report. In addition, Bob has contributed photographs to International Wildlife, Oceans Calendar, Connecticut's Finest and a variety of others, including textbooks. He teaches underwater photography courses and lectures on the marine life of the Northeast.

Foreword

Diver-authors who write about a favorite shipwreck, whet the appetite yet seldom give its exact location. It was in response to this frustration that I set out to write SCUBA NORTHEAST. Volume II is a revision and expansion of Volume I to include selected shipwrecks and dive sites of Rhode Island to New Jersey. As much as possible, the exact position of wrecks, via Loran C. has been included in the book. Though not all of the Loran positions furnished by a variety of sources were confirmed by me, (something that could have taken a lifetime of diving with our short season), most are accurate within reason. Wrecks of course, are not the sole reason that many of us dive. The northeast waters also harbor a profuse and diverse marine life, giving sightseers, underwater photographers and "food collectors" additional reason for pursuing this great sport.

Robert G. Bachand

NORTHEAST DIVING

Pink flowerlike hydroids and brightly colored shell-less snails, nudibranchs, as pretty as any found on Australia's Great Barrier Reef, decorate the rock reefs. Dark red sea stars and foot tall anemones cling to the stone surfaces. Schools of fish patrol the reefs with patches of small star corals scattered throughout the area. The Caribbean? Not at all; it's the coastal waters of Southern New England, New York and New Jersey.

Beginning with the waters off New Jersey and the south shore of Long Island, extending through Long Island Sound to the coast of Rhode Island and Block Island, divers will find a surprising variety of delicate marine life forms. With the incursion of the Gulf Stream in late summer, these areas are occasionally host to juvenile tropical fish. The first time this diver ran into a four-eyed butterfly fish at Fort Wetherill, Rhode Island, there was an immediate assumption that it was either a serious case of "morning after" or nitrogen narcosis at the shallow depth of twenty feet! Though octopuses are not normal residents of our coast, there were two recorded off Long Island in 1945. Temperature and salinity however prevent these more exotic southern residents from becoming permanently established in our waters. Nevertheless, there are tremendous numbers of interesting and pretty local marine animals.

1

The May 9, 1909 issue of the New York Times reported 1,076 marine disasters along coastal Rhode Island to the tip of Cape Cod, occurring in just a 60 year period! Over 100 wrecks are charted on Long Island Sound with probably ten times that figure being a more realistic number since Adrian Block first sailed the Sound in 1614. The bottom of the Sound is described by Jeannette Rattray in her book, (Perils of the Port of New York,New York, Dodd Mead, 1973) as being paved with coal,.. "a legacy of a time when schooners and long 'strings' of barges, towed by a single tug, traveled the sometimes unforgiving waters." Coastal New Jersey (293 wrecks occurred from 1849-1871) and the south shore of Long Island, with their approaches to New York Harbor, certainly rank high with others in the number of shipwrecks. Most of those were due to storms, fog, strandings, collisions and enemy action during the two World Wars.

The Defense, a privateer believed to have been carrying as much as $500,000 in gold and silver, is thought to have sunk on Bartlett's Reef, in Long Island Sound. In 1780, the HMS Hussar, a British pay ship, carrying up to $4 million in gold and silver, sank in New York's East River. The majority of wrecks however, offer the diver a spirit of adventure, a look at history and marine life, and some souvenirs, but little chance of success as a true treasure hunter.

THE TIDES

Some eight thousand years ago, Long Island Sound was a fresh water lake. As the seas rose, fresh and salt waters mixed and marine creatures began their invasion. With the incursion of the ocean, tides began to influence the Sound. Bounded by the state of New York on the south shore and Connecticut on the north side, the funnel shaped body of water is most narrow at its extreme western end. Because of the peculiar shape of Long Island Sound, the tidal range or difference of water depth between high and low tides is greatest at the western, more narrow end. Thus a diver will find about a 7 foot difference between high and low tides in Stamford, Connecticut, while there is only a change of about 3 feet at New London. (Willets Point, 7 feet, Sand Hook and Rockaway Beach, 4.6 feet, Block Island, 3 feet, Newport, Rhode Island, 3.5 feet). This difference in tidal depths can produce significant changes in water visibility, especially at the western end of Long Island Sound. The extra 7 feet of depth, can help prevent waves from "kicking up" the bottom on a more shallow dive.

DIVING DEPTHS

The average depth of Long Island Sound is only 60 feet with a maximum of 306 feet, near the extreme eastern end. Most diving in Long Island Sound is probably done in depths of 10 to 30 feet, though wreck divers plunge from 40 to 90 feet. At those depths in Long Island Sound, visibility can be nil, making those excursions necessarily fro only the very experienced. Dive sites and wrecks off New Jersey, New York and Rhode Island included in the book, range from very shallow to beyond normal sport diver's depth. Diving any of the sites should be planned according to training and experience.

CURRENTS

Tides cause our currents, with wind and wave action adding to their strength. The currents which are generated can be dangerous to the unwary diver. There are particularly strong currents at Orient Point, the Race and over popular wrecks such as the Onondaga and the Larchmont. The maximum current velocity at the Race is about 5 knots (6 mph; 1 knot=1.15 mph). Before diving a new area, it is best to consult tidal charts, then look for signs of current at the site. Lobster pot floats can give a hint of the strength of the current. Swirling water around the line or a float being "dragged down," are sure indications of a strong current. Buoys can also be similarly observed. If the dive float or flag moves away from the boat in the absence of wind, the diver should suspect the presence of a current. Points of land extending out into the water, river mouths and constricting narrows, are all likely sites for strong currents.

The effects and dangers of currents can be minimized by diving, at or near, slack high or low tide. At the moment that the tide changes direction, there is usually little movement of water, thus a "slack" period. The length of the slack period can be different for different areas. In most cases however, currents during that time are slow moving enough to be easily manageable for about one half hour on either side of peak high or low tide. Thus, this gives a diver about one hour bottom time.

If unsure of a current or you are entering a known strong current, it is best to dive with a tether line. The tether is tied to the anchor line, boat or some other secure spot; the other end held by the diver. The same device can be used in low visibility water while searching for a wreck or a mooring. A long trailing float tied to the boat is another safety feature which should be used in case divers emerge downstream of the boat. If caught in a current, walking hand-over-hand on the bottom, grasping rocks as you go, is useful for getting out of a difficult situation. Even more important however, someone should stay aboard the boat, watching for those who might get into difficulty.

As waves break on the beach, the piled-up water must somehow make its way back out. It moves out in narrow bands of strong currents known as a rip or undertow. These currents, seldom more than 10 to 20 feet wide, can attain velocities of 4 to 5 mph. A diver caught in a rip current should not try to fight it by attempting to swim back to shore. Instead, swim across the current and parallel to the beach.

VISIBILITY

Fully one third of the reduction in water visibility in Long Island Sound and throughout the area, is due to microscopic drifting plants known as phytoplankton. Each day, the currents in Long Island Sound pick up and redeposit an estimated seven million tons of sediment, further degrading clarity. At the more narrow western end of Long Island Sound and near river mouths, visibility is the poorest. In general, as you proceed west to east, water clarity improves with the New York side of the Sound usually better than the Connecticut shoreline. This difference is probably due to major rivers draining on the Connecticut shore and the composition of the sea bottom. The bottom along the Connecticut shore is mostly fine sand or silt whereas New York's consists of a heavier, coarse sand, which is not as easily picked up in stormy waters and settles out sooner. On the south shore of Long Island, New Jersey and coastal Rhode Island, onshore winds produce waves which pick up sediment and decrease visibility.

In most years, throughout the area, visibility is best during the colder months, provided that the seas have remained calm. Spring diving is good, though visibility can be greatly reduced in late February or early March, due to a phytoplankton bloom. During the summer, Long Island Sound offers its best clarity from about mid July to mid August, especially after a period of no rain and calm seas. During times of a Bermuda high, the water is usually at its best. Block Island, offshore Rhode Island, the south shore of Long Island and New Jersey clear up considerably in late summer and early fall as the area is bathed by the incursion of the Gulf Stream.

Some of the best shallow water, late summer diving can be had in the early morning hours, after a night of calm seas. A diver willing to get out of bed for an early morning slack high tide, will be rewarded with some of the best possible water visibility.

WATER TEMPERATURES

Water temperatures throughout the area vary from a low of 32° F. (0°C) in the winter to over 72° F, (22° C) in late summer. (Shallow bays warm and cool sooner than open water). A diver will encounter thermoclines on deeper dives, especially off Block Island, coastal Rhode Island, New Jersey and the south shore of Long Island. A one quarter inch Farmer John with a hood and chicken vest is usually adequate for most, from about mid-May to early November. "Long John" underwear, top and bottom, worn under a wet suit (over the chicken vest) will help reduce water flow in cold water. Pouring warm water into a wet suit just before entering the water, can also help conserve body heat for a time. It is however, more comfortable and safer to wear a dry suit from December to May or when making an extended deep water summer dive into a thermocline.

Lobstering

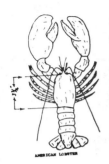

Lobstering, a favorite activity for many divers, is available via permit to residents and in some states, non-residents. Capturing a lobster is generally easier at night when the creature is out of its den. However it can be done during the day. Massachusetts in fact, permits lobster diving only during daylight hours. Rhode Island, Connecticut, New York and New Jersey have presently no such restriction. (Regulations have changed considerably over the years, thus check with the state authorities).

Day or night, a light is always useful for examining a lobster den. An occupied den often has fresh sand or gravel pushed out in front of it. If a lobster is in its den, shine the light just ahead of it and the crustacean will usually move out a bit to investigate. A light directed into a "bug's" eyes, will send it back farther into its hole. The crustacean prefers to occupy a tight fitting burrow. This allows it to wedge itself with its legs, claws and rostrum (the long spine between its eyes). When you have established that a lobster is in a den, thrust a *gloved* hand into the hole, pinning down the claw(s), and slowly work up the claws until you have the critter by the body. Turning the creature slightly side to side will ordinarily dislodge it. It is sometimes necessary, however, to dig out from under the lobster, to free it from its home. Trying to pull it out of its burrow by just a claw will usually get you just that, a claw (s). When in that type of situation, the lobster has the ability to throw a claw (s) (autotomy), as it does if it encounters a problem while shedding its old shell. Though lost parts do regenerate and return to the normal size, a lobster without claws, probably has little chance of survival.

At night, the lobster roams about in search of food. Shine the light just ahead of the "bug" and grab it from behind with the other hand. "Keepers" must be 3 3/16 inches in length as measured by placing a gauge at the back of the eye socket to the end of the body shell (beginning of the tail). Be sure to check for eggs under the tail.

☞ Minimum lobster body shell length, 3 1/4 in : 1991

If a female has eggs, known as "in berry", release it. Eggs may not be scrubbed or otherwise removed. Heavy fines for not complying, not to mention the shortsighted loss of a future generation, should be a sufficient deterrent.

Spearing or snagging lobster is not permitted in any of the states. "Bugs" should be handled with care for a very obvious reason; large crusher claws can break a finger!

Blue crab

The blue crab may be taken In Connecticut, New York and Rhode Island by residents without a license, from May 1 through November 30th. Size limit in Connecticut and New York is 5 inches

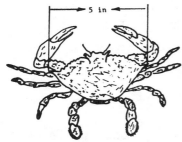

from point to point on the body shell; 4 1/8 inches in Rhode Island. Soft shell crabs must be at least 3.5 inches, point to point in Connecticut. Egg bearing females cannot be taken in any of the states. The orange mass of eggs (black when near to hatching), is carried on the underside of the crab. The female blue crab can carry up to two million eggs though only about 1% of the hatched larvae ever survive to become juveniles. The blue crab is generally found in salt marshes, bays, or near river mouths in shallow water. The crustacean is most common at the eastern end of Long Island Sound, the south shore of Long Island, New Jersey and Rhode Island waters with very few at the western end of Long Island Sound. The creature can be taken from the surface by baited line, dip net, or folding trap. Divers who take blue crab by hand border on being somewhat masochistic. The crab is very aggressive, pinching without mercy. If a diver breaks off a claw in desperation, instead of relaxing as it does with the lobster, the severed appendage contracts further, squeezing the unfortunate even harder! Under those circumstances a diver quickly learns how to scream underwater. Trying to stuff the captured crab into a game bag while you are still in the water, is asking for even more trouble from the agile swimmer; *but it sure tastes great!*

Another species of swimming crab that resides in our area is the lady crab or calico crab. It is usually found near shore, in shallow water, often buried to its eye stalks in sand. Like the blue crab, this crustacean is feisty and well equipped to defend itself. A real dive buddy is one who pries the stubborn little crab's claw off your finger as you are biting through the mouthpiece on your regulator! The crab is edible and quite tasty but because of its size, it offers little "meat".

The similar looking rock crab and jonah crab are also edible; the jonah crab is the larger of the two. The jonah is mostly found in deeper water while the rock crab inhabits the shallow, near shore waters. Presently, Rhode Island, Connecticut and New York do not regulate the taking of lady, rock or jonah crabs. It is however, illegal to take an egg-bearing female of any species.

PERMITS

State of Connecticut, Department of Environmental Protection, State Office Bldg., Hartford, Ct. 06115

State of New York, Department of Environmental Conservation, Building 40, State University of New York, Stony Brook, N.Y. 11794

State of Rhode Island, Department of Environmental Management, Divisions of Enforcement, 83 Park St., Providence, R. I. 02903

State of New Jersey, no permit required for residents or non-residents.

Probably the most dangerous marine animal encountered in local waters, is the careless diver himself. Beyond this fellow, few if any dangerous creatures lurk in area depths.

Oyster toadfish, *Opsanus tau:* A few publications on dangerous marine animals refer to the toadfish, as venomous. It is probably confused with a near relative which resides in the Pacific. As confirmed by H.E. Winn, a University of Rhode Island researcher on the oyster toadfish, the creature is not venomous. It does nevertheless have spines on its sides and back which can penetrate the skin if handled improperly.

Jellyfish: One of the more commonly seen jellyfish throughout the area is the lion's mane, *Cynea capillata* (see photo, page 10). Averaging about one foot in diameter, the same species is known to grow in the Artic to an incredible size of eight feet in diameter, with two hundred foot tentacles! In this area it is seen mostly in the spring and late summer. For individuals who are particularly sensitive to its sting, contact with the lion's mane is potentially dangerous. For most however, the response ranges from a minor irritation to an itchy rash, lasting up to one week. As with other jellyfish, a wet suit, jeans, thin gloves etc., are sufficient to prevent stings.

The color of the lion's mane varies from pink to yellow-orange. It is a great subject for underwater photographers, especially when it harbors young butterfish. These juveniles swim without harm, in and out of the jellyfish's protective umbrella.

The sea nettle, *Chrysoara quinquecirrha,* (try to pronounce that in one breath!) is a small, milky-white jellyfish that stings far out of proportion to its size. (see photo, page 26) Well known for its sting in the Chesapeake Bay, where it is often drives swimmers out of the water, it is found mostly in shallow, brackish water along this coast.

The Portuguese man-of-war, *Physalia physalia,* with its purple balloonlike float, is sometimes seen along the coast. The rare visitor is transported by the Gulf Stream sometimes as far north as the Gulf of Maine. Its sting, which is said to feel like a hot poker, is

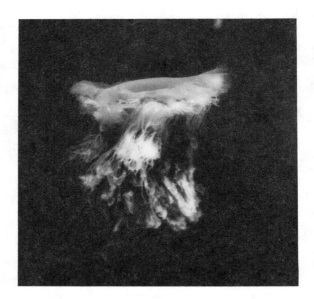

Lions mane jellyfish, *Cyanea capillata*, L.I.S.

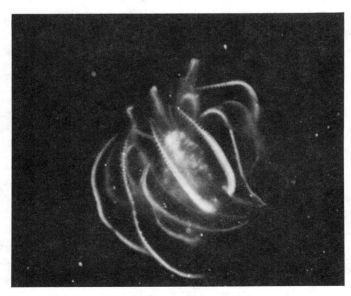

Comb jelly, *Mneiopsis leidyi*, 1:3, Block Island Sound

potentially very dangerous for some individuals. Even a beached specimen, in the hot sun, retains its stinging power for a long time.

The comb jelly, though usually seen throughout the diving season, occurs in great hordes by late August. The marine animal is not a true jellyfish and has no stinging cells; thus it is not harmful to humans. Propelled by a constant beating of its "combs", the comb jelly makes a great subject for photographs. The combs produce a rainbow-like effect when struck by the light of an electronic flash. (see photo, page 10)

Treatment for jellyfish stings consist of immediate application of alcohol, witch hazel, perfume, beer (what a waste), meat tenderizer or vinegar. The tentacles should not be washed off with fresh water or rubbed off. This will only trigger the discharge of other stinging cells, (nematocysts). Cortisone creams, lotions or sprays are helpful in reducing swelling. In more severe cases, a physician should be consulted.

Redbeard sponge: Redbeard sponge *Microcione prolifera,* a very common, pretty, local sponge, can cause a rare skin rash or contact dermatitis. Known as red moss poisoning, it can produce redness and stiffness of the fingers with swelling of the hands. A physician should be consulted if so afflicted.

Sharks, skates & rays: Sharks are normal residents of all seas, thus it should not be surprising that local waters harbor their own variety. In the event of an encounter with a shark, the diver should take appropriate action, "get the h— out of the water!" According to the conclusions of the Sears Foundation for Marine Research, the danger of shark attack, although existent, is so exceedingly remote as to be negligible in temperate seas. This is true unless it is known that a dangerous variety of shark is in the vicinity. This statement does not hold up, of course, when speaking of warmer waters where a large concentration of sharks reside.

Next to the spiny and smooth dogfish, the sand shark, *Carcharias taurus,* is probably the most common species of shark in the area. The shark is generally first sighted in late May and remains until October. There are no records of attack on humans by this shark in North America. Its near relative in East Indian waters however, is a known man eater. The brown shark, also known as the sandbar shark, *Carcharhinus milberti*, is found in shallow bays and harbors where females give birth to their young. The shark is common to Block Island and the bays of Long Island Sound. It feeds primarily on flounder, eel, crab and shellfish. It has never been known to attack man.

The list of sharks entering area waters is by no means complete. Requiem sharks, such as the mako and blue are seen yearly with the great white making occasional forays to the area. Their presence should be enough to keep divers temporarily out of the water.

The roughtail stingray, *Dasyatis centroura*, normally a resident of warmer waters, is a seasonal visitor to this region. It arrives sometime in June or July, remaining until early October. Though it is highly unlikely that a diver would come into contact with a stingray, its tail, which is equipped with spines as long as five inches, could potentially inflict serious wounds. Growing to a wingspan of nearly five feet, the marine animal is related to skate and shark.

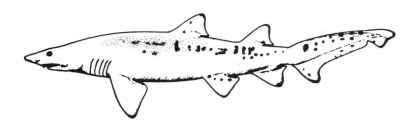

Sand Shark, *Carcharias taurus*

Sand shark, Carcharias taurus. Block Island

Barndoor skate, *Raja laevis*. Long Island Sound

Only the more common marine fish likely to be seen by a diver will be mentioned. It is not in the scope of this book, to cover all of the marine fish indigenous to the area.

American eel, *Anguilla rostrata:* The American eel is most often

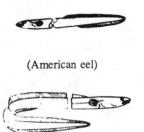

(American eel)

(Conger eel)

encountered at night. Growing 2 to 4 feet in length, it is ordinarily found in the vicinity of rocks or a wreck. Its color varies according to the bottom on which it dwells; dark, when it lives on mud, pale, when on sand. An eel over 24 inches is probably a female; mature males are 12 to 18 inches. The eel is easy to photograph since it is "frozen" by a diver's light. The curious creature can even be lured out into the open for a better picture. Spearfishing divers may enjoy eating what is said to be a good tasting marine animal. The American eel is less aggressive than the look-alike conger eel. It is distinguished from the latter by its long lower jaw which sticks out beyond the upper jaw.

Rock eel, *Pholis gunnellus:* The rock eel which averages only 6 to

8 inches in length, is usually found in shallow water between and under rocks and dead shells. It is an easy subject of underwater photographers.

Eelpout, *Macrozoarces americanus:* "Old blubberlips" as it is

sometimes referred to, it is also known as the congo eel, ling, snakefish, rock eel and muttonfish. It is commonly seen on New Jersey and Long Island south shore wrecks, especially hiding under debris. The eelpout is a good subject for underwater photographers, since it seldom moves unless approached too abruptly. It is also fair game for spearfishermen. Unfortunately, the flesh has numerous blotches caused by parasites, making it unappetizing.

Sandlaunce, *Ammodytes americanus:* The American sandlaunce lives on sandy bottoms, avoiding rocky areas. Burrowed in the sand, it "flies"  out of the sea floor in great numbers, just ahead of an intruding diver. Out of reach, it dives back to the safety of the sand bottom. Though fairly common throughout the area, it is consistently seen at Eaton's Neck, Long Island Sound. The eel-like fish averages between 4 to 6 inches and is food for larger fish such as cod, silver hake, striped bass and blue fish.

Northern pipefish, *Syngnathus fuscus:* The pipefish reside near shore, in very shallow water, It has the ability to swim both horizontally and  vertically as does its close relative, the trumpet fist. It is also related to the sea horse, cornet fish and the snipe fish. Averaging 4 to 8 inches, the pipefish is usually seen in eelgrass or seaweed.

Grubby, *Myoxocephalus aeneus:* This very common fish lives in shallow water to 90 feet. Rarely exceeding a length of 6 inches, it thus is  ideal for macro photography. Though it can be photographed during the day, it is easier to approach at night, when it is less active. A 1:2 extension tube on a 35 mm Nikonos lens, produces an excellent close-up photo.

Searobin, *Prionotus carolinus & P. evolans:* Divers can observe the searobin with its large fanlike fins from the shoreline to deep dives. As it  moves along the bottom, it seems to walk with the fleshy feelers near its head. A diver will often find it buried to its eyes, in a sandy bottom. The robin is difficult to approach but makes award-winning photos if the flash catches its emerald colored eyes. The searobin is a noisy sound-producer, especially when disturbed or taken out of the water. Its flesh is tasty, firm, white and similar to that of whiting.

Sea raven, *Hemitripterus americanus:* The color of the odd-looking fish, varies from red, yellow to brown. It is very common on deep wrecks such as the U-853 and others around Block Island. During the colder months, it is apt to be found in shallow

water. The sea raven deposits its eggs at the base of finger sponge and crumb-of-bread sponge, from October to January, its spawning season. The eggs are similar in color to the sponge, thus they are effectively camouflaged. The fish is easy to photograph since even when it swims away, it seldom moves too far.

Goosefish, *Lophius americanus:* The goosefish, also known as the angler fish and monkfish, ranks with the sea raven and oyster toadfish for pure ugliness. The goosefish "baits" its prey with a lure attached to the top of its head. In a blinding snap, it swallows its victim. Its diet is said to consist of

anything from a wide variety of fish to small buoys and an occasional seabird. Growing to a length of 4 to 5 feet, it has been recorded weighing as much as 70 pounds! The fish is most often encountered on the south shore of Long Island and Block Island Sound. Its range is from Newfoundland to Brazil. The flesh of the goosefish, long served in the kitchens of Europe, has gained some acceptance in the U. S. It is marketed under the name of monkfish.

Squirrel hake, *Urophycis chuss:* The squirrel hake, also called hake and ling, is common on the deeper area wrecks. Interestingly, its young of 1-2.5 inches, spend their time living inside the mantle of deep sea scallops. A

relative of cod, the adult grows from 1 to 3 pounds.

Tomcod, *Microgadus tomcod:* The tomcod very closely resembles a  small cod (they are related) with its barbel on the chin and its codlike fins. The fish feeds on small crabs, fish, clams and worms. It lives near the coastline, often entering fresh water. Common in Long Island Sound, the tomcod is shy and usually difficult to photograph.

Threadfin, *Alectis crinitus:* The threadfin is a summer stray in northeast waters. The small fish of 3 to 4 inches in length, has long threadlike fins extending to 7 inches. Though rare, this diver has seen it in small schools, on two separate occasions, at the Pinnacle, off Block Island.

Cunner, *Tautogolabrus adspersus:* The cunner or bergall, is the  most common marine fish seen by divers. Deep or shallow, it is always present. The fish prefers rock reefs or any suitable hiding place. At shallow depths, it is generally no longer than 4 to 6 inches. On deep wrecks, it can measure up to 15 inches. The longest recorded cunner was 17.5 inches, weighing over 3 pounds. It was caught on September 9, 1953 in New Brunswick, Canada. At night, the fish sleeps with its dorsal (back) fin extended. A diver's light will often send it scurrying.

Blackfish, *Tautog onitis:* The blackfish or tautog is closely related to the cunner, Spanish hogfish and many others in the wrasse  family. The young blackfish has three pairs of dark bars on its sides; the adult is nearly entirely black. Like the cunner however, its color varies with its habitat. The blackfish is a favorite target for spearfishing divers. It ranges in size from 1 to 6 pounds; the record specimen caught weighed 22.5 pounds. The usual haunt for blackfish are breakwalls, lighthouse rocks, rock reefs, bridge abutments and shallow shipwrecks. At night, the fish lies dormant, wedged between rocks. A light, shined directly into its eyes, will spook the blackfish, leaving behind a cloud of sediment. A normal resident of the area throughout the year, the blackfish moves to deeper water during the winter where some believe it to hibernate.

Striped bass, *Morone saxatilis:* The striped bass is usually seen by

divers around rocks or shipwrecks. It is fast, thus difficult to photograph or spear. Since all of the states have regulations specific to its capture, be sure to check the local laws.

Flounders, Order *Heterosomata*-flatfishes: All species of flatfish begin life as other fish, with eyes on each side of the head. As the juvenile matures, one eye migrates to the other side; an adaptation of its sea bottom life. With the exception of the small mouth flounder whose maximum length is 4 inches, flats are a good catch for divers.

winter flounder
Pseudopleuronectes americanus

summer flounder - fluke
Paralichthys dentatus

windowpane flounder
Scophthalmus aquosus

hogchoker
Trinectes maculatus

They are easily speared with just a dive knife or can be caught by hand. They can sometimes be attracted to a diver by striking two rocks together, underwater. At night, flats are stunned by a diver's light, making them easy to photograph. None are known for a great IQ but by far the dumbest has to be the hogchoker, family Soleidae. (It is not in the same family as the flounder). The hogchoker can easily be caught by hand. Though not particularly photogenic, it often can be moved to a different location for a better picture. Despite its appearance, it is delicious tasting.

Flatfish are differentiated by the position of their eyes on their head. The summer flounder (fluke), fourspotted flounder, smallmouth flounder and windowpane flounder, all belonging to the same family, Bothidae, are left handed, with both eyes on the left side of the head. The winter flounder's (blackback) eyes are on the right side as are those of the hogchoker.

Ocean sunfish, Mola mola: The *Mola mola* has been known to

enter the eastern end of Long Island Sound.Divers however, are more likely to encounter this unusual open water fish off Block Island or the coast of New Jersey and south shore of Long Island. Resembling a massive pancake, its record size tipped the scales at 4,400 pounds! It is related to puffer fish, porcupine fish and file fish. The Mola's diet is mainly jellyfish, comb jelly and tiny invertebrates.

Other fish sometimes encountered:

porgy - scup
Stenotomus versicolor

black-sea bass
Centropristes striatus

butterfish
Poronotus triacanthus

northern puffer
Sphaeriodes maculatus

The art of finding a wreck, whether charted or uncharted, takes *patience, persistence, research, luck and a lot of time.* The rewards however are well worth the effort. In addition to self satisfaction, valuable artifacts are sometimes found.

For many divers, the most important equipment used to locate a wreck, is a recording depth sounder and a Loran C unit. There are many different types of these on the market, thus it is best to get advice, prior to purchase, from a reliable marine electronics dealer. A good recording depth sounder, must as much as possible, distinguish between normal bottom topography and a possible wreck. (Knowing the characteristics of your unit well, helps interpret the graph) In the absence of a sounder, a grappling hook or some such device can be substituted.

Loran C

A Loran C is next in importance for locating (and re-locating) a charted or known wreck. Unfortunately, the two instruments together do not assure success. The Loran C system utilizes three to five land based transmitters and a receiver aboard the vessel. A master station and a secondary station transmit synchronized signals at precise intervals with the shipboard receiver measuring the small time difference between the two. The time difference (TD) between the two signals is translated by the receiver (a small computer) into a series of number which relate to a position along a line on the chart. When plotted, numbers obtained from another (different) secondary station and master station, will intersect the first line. This gives the operator, the vessel's exact location. Accuracy depends on the sensitivity of the unit, the quality of its installation, the signal strength, the chart and operator. *Repeatable accuracy* for the individual unit, is the most important information obtained from that unit. Once found, a wreck can be re-located over and over again with that unit. **Any Loran C fix obtained from another unit, gives only a good starting point from which a shipwreck can be located.** When searching for a wreck with Loran C numbers acquired from this book or any other source, steer to those numbers, drop a buoy and begin a pattern. Run the boat back and

WRECK SYMBOLS

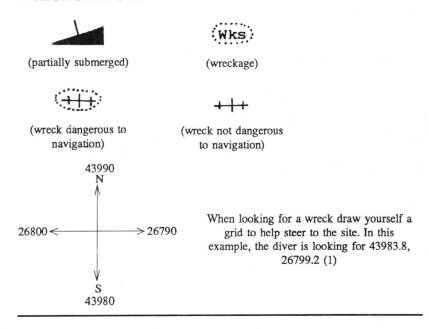

(partially submerged)

(wreckage)

(wreck dangerous to
navigation)

(wreck not dangerous
to navigation)

43990
N

26800 ← → 26790

S
43980

When looking for a wreck draw yourself a
grid to help steer to the site. In this
example, the diver is looking for 43983.8,
26799.2 (1)

forth, parallel to the buoy, using a recording depth finder. The buoy
can be a brightly painted clorox bottle tied to the appropriate length
of line and a lead weight.

More sophisticated devices such as the proton magnetometer
were used in locating the pirate vessel Whydah, sunk off Cape Cod
(1717), and side-scan sonar, used to locate the De Braak off Lewes,
Delaware, lost in 1798. Unfortunately, the costly units are out-of-
reach for most divers. For a more detailed description of how to find
a wreck, see the suggested reading.

Many of the states have or will soon have laws governing the
recovery of artifacts from historically important wrecks. Permits may
be required to remove anything from these sites.

WRECK SAFETY - *the Ascent line*

An ascent line (and/or a penetration/tether line) should be
standard safety equipment for any wreck or deep dive. On a
decompression dive, it becomes paramount when the anchor line
cannot be relocated due to low visibility or current. Secure one end

of the line to the wreck and play out line as you ascend. Caught away from the boat in a current, tie the line to your weight belt, drop it, and use it as an anchor.

UNDERWATER PHOTOGRAPHY

There are two main requirements for successful photography in northeast waters. The first, a good understanding of close-up and wide angle photo techniques, the second, some knowledge of the natural history of the marine animals to be photographed. Though it is not the purpose of this book to teach underwater photography, suggestions will be made applicable especially to low visibility water.

Available light photography   (photography without the aid of artificial light)

Available light photography, because of the rapid lost of ambient light in low visibility area water, is necessarily restricted to the shallows. The best time of day to shoot available light, is during the hours of 10 AM to 2 PM, when the sun is at its highest peak. High speed film (eg. 400 ASA), is also necessary for this type of photography. As you move farther away from the subject, sediment in the water causes the rapid loss of picture sharpness. Thus, a rule of thumb, should be: the greater the amount of sediment, the closer the photographer must be to the subject. (That is also vary true for flash photography). A 28mm wide angle lens, preferably a 20mm or a 15mm, on a Nikonos camera allows a marine photographer to be close, yet cover a wide area. In addition to staying close, avoid shadow areas since those usually produce disappointing, "flat" pictures without the light of a flash.

Jellyfish near the surface, such as the lion's mane and moon jelly, make good subjects for available light. Dramatic pictures can be produced by getting the jellyfish in the foreground with the sun in the background (backlighting). For maximum contrast, take the light reading from the sun. Shallow wrecks, such as the Onondaga which lies in 50 feet of water off Rhode Island, are appropriate subjects when the water is clear.

Flash photography *(strobes)*

In low visibility water, backscatter caused by particulate matter in the water can completely obliterate a photo, giving you the feeling that it was taken in a raging snowstorm! Even just a small amount of backscatter can ruin an otherwise great picture. To minimize the effect, the strobe must be aimed in such a way that the subject is receiving most of the lighting, avoiding the foreground and background as much as possible. That can be accomplished by lighting the subject with a *hand -held* flash, above, and to the side, at about 45°. Try shooting several photos at different angles, since moving the strobe even slightly can make quite a difference. (A strobe held too low, next to the framer, will cast the shadow of the framer in the picture). Lighting the subject from directly behind the camera will light all of the particles between the subject and the camera, producing the snowstorm effect. Just as important however, is the distance to the subject. Again, greater the sediment, closer the subject must be. In low visibility water, a flash photo should be taken at a distance of less than 1/4 the distance that you can see. If visibility is 4 to 5 feet, limit photographs to one foot or less. *Always err on the side of being closer.*

Staying close is possible by using a wide angle lens, extension tube, supplementary lens or a macro lens. An extension tube is a hollow tube that is placed between the lens and camera body. A progressively longer tube, will produce a progressively greater magnification and a shorter subject to camera distance. Extension tubes generally come in magnifications of 1:1 (life size), 1:2 (1/2 life size), 1:3 (1/3 life size) and occasionally 2:1 (2X life size). The supplementary close-up lens is placed directly on the front of the camera's lens, giving a magnification of about 1:5 (1/5 life size). With any of these devices, always set the camera's lens at f/22, for maximum depth of field. (Depth of field, simply defined, is the picture area that is in focus).

Swimming into a current helps keep kicked-up sediment behind you. If possible, photograph in a "quiet" area, between wreck structure or rocks.

Natural history

Water temperatures along the coastline vary tremendously from about 32° F in the winter, to about 72 to 74° F in the summer. Local marine animals have adapted to this range, each with its own particular mechanism. Winter flounder and tomcod, for instance, have an antifreeze protein which lowers the freezing point of their body fluids, allowing them to flourish in cold water. Many of the flowerlike hydroids (related to jellyfish, coral and anemones), do best at lower temperatures. As the surface waters begin warm, these hydroids disappear from the shallows and are then found only at the colder depths. Other animals, because of food requirements, are found only in certain locations or are more common at one site than another. Thus, knowing when and where to look for specific creatures is a second requirement for getting a variety of good photos in northeast waters.

The following describes briefly when and where to find some of the marine animals, including suggestions on what equipment to use.

1. *Red beard sponge, Microciona prolifera:* Look for this red to orange sponge at shallow depths, on pilings, rocks and any hard surface. It is found throughout the area especially in late summer.

    Suggestions: 1:5, 1:3

2. *Yellow boring sponge, Cliona* species: It is often found on the bottom, in large clumps, covering rocks or oyster shells during the entire summer.

    Suggestions: 1:5 to 1:1. The sponge is highly reflective, thus easy to overexpose. Vary the exposure (bracket) by holding the strobe at different distances from the subject.

3. *Finger sponge, Haliclona oculata:* These species of sponge are easiest to find early in the season, before kelp and other seaweed have overgrown dive sites. They are found in shallow water to about 40 feet.

    Suggestions: 1:5, 1:3

3. *Hydroids:* The pink hearted flowerlike hydroid, *Tubularia crocea,* is the most conspicuous of this family of marine animals. The animal begins to disappear when the water temperature reaches 55 to 58° F. It is then found only in deeper, colder water. (See Miner, R.W. in the suggested reading, for the best illustration of the pink hearted hydroid)

    Suggestions: 1:5 to 2:1 In general, the higher magnifications produce the most pleasing photo of the hydroid.

4. *Anemone:* The frilled anemone, *Metridium senile,* is the most common of the area's anemones. The best time to photograph it, is at night, (or on a deep wreck) when/(where) it is fully expanded.

    Suggestions: 1:5 to 1:1, 28mm, 20mm or 15mm wide angle

lens. Try backlighting using a slave.

5. **Star coral,** *Astrangia danea:* The northern star coral is the only stony coral found in area waters. The small coral is common throughout the northeast, from the shore to 120 feet. Unlike most Caribbean corals, its polyps (the living part of the animal) are expanded both day and night. For a different type of picture, touch the polyp lightly with the framer and take the photo as the coral begins to retract.

Suggestions: 1:5 to 1:1 Highly reflective, bracket

6. **Soft coral,** *Alcyonium digitatum:* It is found in fairly shallow water at Fort Wetherill, Rhode Island and in deep water only off the coast of New Jersey. Known as "dead man's fingers," it is nocturnal with its polyps retracted during the day, except in subdued light.

Suggestions: 1:3, 1:2 Highly reflective, bracket

7. **Sea nettle,** *Chrysaora quinquecirrha:* Look for this beautiful little stinger (up to 4 inches), in quiet bays and tidal marshes. The jelly fish tend to "pile up" on the windward side of a bay. Cover all exposed areas of the skin since its sting can be more than annoying.

Suggestions: 1:5 to 1:2 Bracket

8. **Lion's mane,** *Cyanea capillata:* Seen in small numbers during the spring and in large swarms in late summer. In late August, look for juvenile butterfish which seek protection under the jellyfish's umbrella. It is easiest to photograph in quiet bays.

Suggestions: Available light or strobe. 35mm, 28mm, 20mm, or 15mm lens.

9. **Comb jellies:** Common during most of the diving season. (see page 9)

Suggestions: 1:5 (personal favorite), 1:3

10. **Nudibranch:** *Coryphella* species: It is probably the prettiest creature that lives on our shore. It is found only in colder water. (During the spring in Long Island Sound and Rhode Island waters.) Look among hydroids upon which it feeds.

Suggestions: 1:1, 2:1

11. **Blue eyed (bay) scallop** *Aequipecten irradians:* It is found in eelgrass and a variety of bottoms from the low tide line to 50 feet. Often seen at Niantic Bay in Long Island Sound and in bays on the south shore of Long Island and Rhode Island.

Suggestion: 1:3 to 1:1

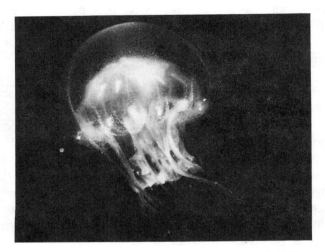

Sea nettle, *Chrysaora quinquecirrha*, **1:3, LIS**

Nudibranch, shell-less snail, *Coryphella* **sp., 1:1, LIS**

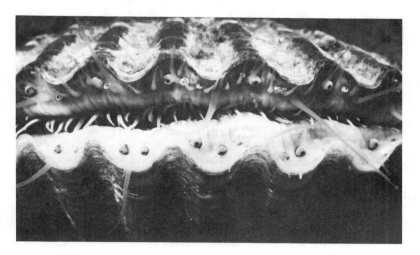

Blue-eyed (bay) scallop, *Aquipecten irradians*, 1:3, LIS

Hermit crab, *Pagarus longicarpus*, 1:1, New Jersey

Pink-hearted hydroid, *Tubularia crocea*, 2:1, R.I.

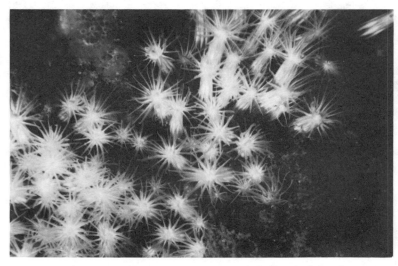

Lined anemone, *Fagesia lineata*, 1:3, Block Island

Winter flounder, *Pseudopleuronectes americanus,* **1:3, N.Y.**

Fan worm (orange color) *Serpulid* **sp., 2:1, Mystic, Ct.**

29

Mantis shrimp, *Squilla empusa***, 1:3, Narragansett Bay**

Newborn toadfish, *Opsanus tau***, 1:1, Long Island Sound**

12. *Sea stars:* The common sea star, *Asterias forbesii*, is seen throughout Long Island Sound. The boreal star, *A. vulgaris*, is usually only found at the extreme eastern end of Long Island Sound off Block Island. The deep red blood star, *Henrecia sanguinolenta*, prefers the cold waters of Rhode Island, eastern Long Island Sound and deeper waters off the south shore of Long Island and New Jersey.

Suggestions: 1:5 to 1:3

13. *Feather duster worms:* The pretty little orange, red, purple or tan creatures find a home on dock pilings, the underside of rocks and any other hard surface. Their small size makes them hard to locate. They are often expanded on overcast days or at night.

Suggestions: 1:1 or 2:1 (2:1 best because of their very small size)

14. *Hermit crab, Pagurus sp.* It is the easiest of the crustaceans to photograph. As soon as it is approached or picked up, it quickly disappears to the safety of its shell. Find some soft sand, make a small mound and place the crab on top of it. Position the camera's framer at eye level so that when the creature emerges from the shell, it will be staring directly into the lens. Try it a few times, the photos are worth it.

Suggestions: 1:3 to 1:1 depending upon its size.

15. *Lobster and crab* Find an undersized lobster, turn it upside down and let it tire itself flipping its tail. Dig out a slight hollow under a rock and let it back itself in. It will usually stay there long enough to get a photo. At times, you might be lucky to find it out of, or partially emerged, from its den. Jonah, rock and small spider crabs are usually more cooperative than the lobster. If necessary, tire them out as you would a lobster. Good luck with blue, lady and large spider crabs! They are especially aggressive and usually unappreciative of your efforts.

Suggestions: 1:5, 1:3

16. *Mantis shrimp: Squilla empusa:* The mantis shrimp is a crustacean that, in these waters, is at the extreme end of its northern range. During the summer, it digs a shallow u-shaped burrow with two entrances. As the winter approaches and the water temperature drops toward 46° F, it produces a 13 foot deep, vertical burrow! The creature with its spearlike claws and periscopelike eyes is common at

Fort Wetherill, Rhode Island and a number of sites in Long Island Sound. Look for a hole of about 1.5 to 2 inches across, in a mud bottom. If you get lucky, you will find a mantis out of its burrow. Watch out for the claws!

Suggestions: 1:5, 1:3 or wide angle lens.

17. *Seahorse, Hippocampus sp.* The seahorse is not much of a swimmer. It clings with its prehensile tail to eelgrass and seaweed, where it waits for passing food. The fascinating creature is quite common on oyster beds at the western end of Long Island Sound.

Suggestions: 1:5, 1:3

Other fish: see section on common marine fish

Summary of underwater techniques

1. Available light: stay shallow, close to the subject, and avoid shadows. Use high speed films.

2. Flash photography

   a) stay close, ie, within 1/4 the distance that you can see. (Err on the side of being closer)

   b) aim a hand-held strobe above and at 45° to the subject. Vary position of strobe slightly but never shoot the flash from behind the camera.

3. Swim into the current to make sure that kicked up sediment stays behind.

4. Look for "quiet" area between rocks or underwater structures.

5. Acquire at least a minimal knowledge of the natural history of local marine animals. (see suggested reading)

6. PS: choose a light-footed, patient and understanding dive buddy.

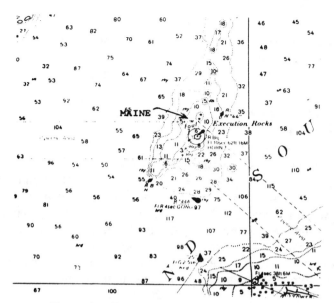

Execution Rocks: wreck of the Maine

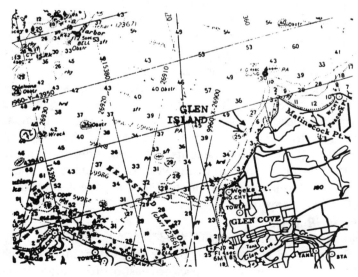

Matinecock Point: Glen Island wreck

33

LONG ISLAND SOUND: northern and southern shores

Beach access diving along coastal Connecticut and the north shore of Long Island (NY) is limited. Divers seeking the best and most varied sites in Long Island Sound, will need a boat or a charter.

EXECUTION ROCKS LIGHT - N.Y.
New Rochelle, N.Y.
Chart #12363, 12366

Standing at the extreme western end of the Sound, Execution Rocks Light is a popular dive site. First built in 1850 and rebuilt in 1868, the facility was manned by the Coast Guard until December 1979 when it became automatic. One legend lends the name of the site to the execution of patriots by the British during the Revolutionary War. The unfortunates were said to have been shackled to the rocks at low tide. Death came slowly, by drowning. Another explanation attributes the name to the many ships lost on the nearby reef. In testimony to this, the wreck of the steamer Maine is just a short distance from the light.

It is best to approach the light from the south, avoiding the treacherous reefs at the northeast corner. From this direction, a boat can be anchored 40 to 50 feet from the lighthouse rocks. The large boulders surrounding the lighthouse form caverns, whose walls are covered with anemones, coral and sponge. By early July, red beard sponge dots the entire area. Cunner, blackfish, flounder and occasional oyster toadfish make their residence among the boulders. Lobstering is usually good early in the season. The best time to dive Execution Rocks is at high tide, in calm seas. Visibility can vary from nil to 10+ feet, dependent upon sea conditions. Hazards include small boat traffic, ocean going vessels, current and underwater debris. With a maximum depth of 20 feet, the site is suitable for any level of diving expertise.

STEAMER MAINE
Chart #12366 (N.Y.)   Loran C: 43937.8   26938.5

Sailing from New York to Bridgeport, Connecticut on February 4, 1920, the steamer ran onto pack ice east off Execution Rocks. The vessel immediately lost power. With a combination of northeast winds and tide, it drifted onto the rocks near the lighthouse. Aground in fifteen feet of water, the passengers were stranded on the ship for 3 days prior to rescue. After surveying the damage, the owners decided that the vessel was beyond repair. It was stripped and burned with much of its metal salvaged. The remains lie 100 yards northeast of the light, almost in a direct line of a tall white pole.

Not much is left of the steamer. Ribs, decking and debris serve as refuge for lobsters, cunner and blackfish. A diver can squeeze through some sections through little of value will be found on this well "picked over" wreck. The best time to dive the Maine is at slack tide. WATCH FOR BOAT TRAFFIC!

GLEN ISLAND   Source: Lada Simek
Chart #12463 (Glen Cove, N.Y.) SCUBA Sports Rite Club
Loran C: 43937.6 26893.6 (see photo page 51)

The 238-foot sidewheel steamer was originally commissioned in 1890 as the City of Richmond. The vessel was later renamed William G. Egerton until converted to an excursion boat by the Starin Line. It was then given the name of Glen Island.

On the evening of December 18, 1904, the steamer entered Long Island Sound, passing Execution Rocks Light as it made its way to its final destination, New Haven, Connecticut. Just off the Great Captain's Light, the Glen Island lost all electrical power. Soon thereafter, smoke and flames leaped up from the decks below. Seeing that his ship was in mortal danger, Captain Charles E. McAllister sounded the alarm and ordered the lifeboats be lowered. Nine lives were lost aboard the vessel. The 22 survivors were picked up by the tug Bully and transferred to the steamer Erasmus Corning. Drifting with the prevailing tides, the burning ship came to rest in 15 to 20 feet of water just inside of Mantinecock Point. The steamer lies about 800 feet offshore, slightly south of a stone mansion. (The structure has 4 chimneys on its main wing and a very high concrete sea wall.) Some of its structure was salvaged, yet plenty remains. A boiler, smoke stack and a number of large timbers, parts of which diver Lada Simek and others believe to be two wrecks (Yacht Vanderbilt?), lie scattered over almost 1/3 acre. The site is residence for some unusually tame blackfish and large schools of cunner. Some artifacts are still occasionally found.

MATINECOCK POINT - N.Y.
Chart #12363, 12366

The coast from Hempstead harbor eastward, is dotted with rock reefs. Matinecock Point has a rock strewn bottom, with many large boulders. Lobstering is good especially in the early season. *Current and boat traffic* are the major hazards of this site.

RYE CLIFF
Source: Walter Blogoslawski, PhD
Chart #12366 (Sea Cliff, N.Y.) National Marine Fisheries Service

Built in Bath, Maine, the 137.5-foot sidewheel paddle steamer was launched on March 22, 1898, bearing the name General Knox. The vessel was used as a railroad ferry until its retirement in 1910. It was then sold to W.H. Perry, converted to an auto ferry, and renamed Rye Cliff. In its new capacity, the vessel operated as an auto ferry between Rye Beach and Sea Cliff. On September 28, 1918, the Rye Cliff caught fire and burned at its Sea Cliff dock. Its remains lie in less than 10 feet of water, about 25 yards W-SW of the rocks, at the south end of Shore Drive, in Sea Cliff. The wreckage consists mainly of timbers, most of which are half buried in the silt. Some brass spikes can still be found with careful inspection of the wreck. Visibility is usually always poor.

SAILBOAT
Source: AWOIS
Chart #12363
NOAA
Lat/Long 42/53/24 73/43/30

The Automated Wreck and Obstruction Information System (AWOIS) reported an 18 foot sailboat in 50 feet of water, 40° and 1900 yards from Execution Rock Light.

UNKNOWN WRECK
Source: AWOIS-1984
Chart #12363
NOAA
Lat/Long 40/53/50 73/43/00

Reported as a probable wreck. *High traffic area.*

SAILBOAT
Source: AWOIS-1984
Chart #12363
NOAA
Lat/Long 43/53/54 73/40/11

A 21-foot sailboat, marked by a buoy, lies in 40 feet of water, just outside of Hempstead Harbor.

COAL BARGE
Source: Lada Simek
Chart #12363
SCUBA Sport Rite Club
Loran C: 43945.7
26930.5

Do you burn coal? A 150-foot long and 50-foot wide coal barge lies in about 40 feet+ of water south off Larchmont. Because much of the structure has deteriorated, the wreck rises to only 3 to 4 feet off the bottom. Some machinery is left on the vessel along with its cargo of coal. Marine life abounds on the wreck. Visibility can range from 5 to 20 feet.

PARSONAGE POINT (Capitol City) Source: Lada Simek
Chart #12363 (Rye N.Y.) SCUBA Sport Rite Club

Parsonage Point, in the town of Rye, New York, has been the site of numerous wrecks. The 250-foot sidewheel steamer Capitol City struck a rock near the point in late March of 1886. Though the wrecked vessel remained above water for nearly a generation, little of it is left at the site. One the west side of the nearby jetty, an unknown wreck has yielded as much as 1200 pounds of lead along with some brass. The jetty often has only a moderate current with visibility of 4 to 20 feet.

FISHING BOAT   Source: Richard Taracka
Chart #12363 (N.Y.)   Greenwich P.D.
Loran C 26946.3 43944.5 (?)

Northwest of Execution Rocks Light. Depth 35 feet.

"SUB" AT BAYVILLE - N.Y.
Chart #12363 Loran: 43938.2 28847.1 (not confirmed)

A barge and parts of what *may* have been a WW I sub, lies slightly east of Reinhard's Restaurant, in Bayville. Local residents take a dim view of divers crossing their property, thus the only real approach is by boat. The wreck(s) are about 150 yards off the beach in 10 to 20 feet of water. The site is occupied by cunner, American eel and some lobster. Visibility is best at a high slack tide with calm seas.

POLING BROTHERS #2-(West)   Source(s) AWOIS-1984
Loran C 26894.8(5.0) 43970.6(7)   Richard Taracka
                                               Bruce Mackin

Built in 1863, the 116-foot oil barge, which is equipped with a pilot house, sank on February 5, 1940, (or possibly March 12, 1940). Lying in 50 feet of water off Great Captain Island, the barge is resting on its keel in a north-south direction. Plenty of souvenirs are left to be found. Watch for netting and fishing line.

POLING BROTHERS (EAST)   Source(s): Bruce Mackin
Chart #12363   Richard Taracka
Loran C: 26864.2 43970.2 (?)

Some controversy exists concerning the identification of the wrecks, Poling Brothers (PB), EAST and WEST. NOAA identified PB WEST as the Poling Brothers #2; local divers believe PB EAST to be the #2. Both are oil barges and both should be dived only by experienced divers. Current can be a problem at any of the mid-Sound wrecks. Always dive at slack tide.

S.E. SPRING &SUGAR BOAT   Source: Richard Taracka
Chart #12367 (Greenwich, Ct.)   Greenwich P.D.
Lat/Long 41/00/32 73/36/51

The excursion boat SE Spring sank in 1903, when it lost control of its rudder and was blown up on the rocks at Meads Point. Located within Greenwich Harbor just off Meads Point, the wreck is easily picked up on a recording depth sounder by running back and forth close, and parallel to, the shoreline. Sitting in 10 feet of water, the wreckage consists of plating, a boiler and some brass, buried under sand and silt.

Remnants of what is believed to be a tug lies in 10 to 15 feet of water, north of Great Captain Island. A barge sits in 15 feet, between Grassy Rocks and Great Captain Rocks.

Typical of so many shallow water wrecks, little remains of the freighter Thames or "Sugar Boat." The ship caught fire on April 25, 1930, two miles off Great Captain Island, and came to rest near Todd Point. A privately maintained buoy, S2A, marks its final resting place. Sitting in only a few feet of water, time, ice and the power of the sea have left little visible evidence of the 560-ton freighter. A few beams remain; the rest is scattered or is buried in the sand.

The wrecked Thames was itself responsible for a number of boating mishaps. On August 1, 1954, a cruiser struck the submerged boiler and sank quickly, never to be located. A second boat collided with the wreck on July 26, 1961 and was also never found.

DREDGING BARGE   Source: Richard Taracka
Chart #12363   Greenwich P.D.
Loran C: 26872.3 60016.4

The dredging barge lies in 77 feet, rising 15 feet off the bottom.

38

Located south of Greenwich Point, most of the machinery remains on the vessel.

GREENWICH POINT PARK-CT.   Source: Richard Taracka
Chart #12363   Greenwich P.D.

The bottom along the east side of Greenwich Point Park is rocky, making it a good area for lobstering. Salvage divers occasionally find old bottles dating back to the area's early settlers. Not accessible via land during the beach season, the area can be approached by boat after first consulting navigational charts. Currents tend to be strong, thus plan to dive at slack tide. Visibility averages 5 feet.

LLOYD NECK-COLD SPRING HARBOR

Source: Gary Nelson
Chart #12365 (N.Y.)   Brent Whitman

The west side of the causeway between Lloyd Neck and Cold Spring harbor is a shallow dive that is especially good for striped bass and blackfish, though poor for lobster. Farther east, at Whitewood Point (NW Bluff), the rock bottom provides numerous places for lobster to hide. Blackfish and striped bass are abundant. At low tide, a diver can walk out on the sandbar at Lloyd Point and work the area between it and Morris Rock. The site is great for weakfish in the spring and blue fish in the fall.

STAMFORD HARBOR BREAKWALL - ISABEL
Chart #12363, 12368

The west breakwall at the entrance of Stamford harbor offers an easy dive to local sport divers. Depth ranges from 7 to 30 feet. The bottom is mostly course sand with small seaweed and sponge covered rocks. Clumps of yellow sulfur sponge are often undermined by lobsters, making them easy pickings. Coral and anemones cover the surfaces of the breakwall. Visibility is best at high tide with calm seas.

Just north of "the Cows" (1000 yards off the east breakwall) lies the remains of the Isabel, a side wheel steamer, which sank in September of 1915.

BLUE HUMMER *(barge)*   Source: Richard Taracka
Chart #12363, 12368 (Stamford, Ct.)   Greenwich P.D.

On February 20, 1934, Long Island Sound was struck by a blizzard. During the night, two barges of the Blue Star Towing Line were lost near Shippan Point. One of the barges, the Blue Hummer, broke up and sank midway between the bell buoy and the lighthouse. Most of its structure lies scattered, with beams, pipes and assorted parts wedged between the rocks.

J-24 (WHERE ARE YOU?)   Source: Skip Crane
Chart 12363 (Darien, Ct.) Oceanic Society
Loran C: 43922.4 26825.7 (last known position)

Sailing out of Noroton Yacht Club on May 23, 1982, a new, yet unnamed, J-24 was within 100 yards of the final buoy in the spring tune-up race.As it sailed downwind in 5 to 7-foot seas, the spinnacker broke loose. Despite efforts by the crew, the 24-foot

vessel breached, the mast touching the water. The crew then climbed over the rail, up to the keel. Compounding the problem, the aft locker had been left open and the sailboat was soon partially filled with water. It then righted itself and the rescued crew watched as their boat sank still under full sail. The Oceanic Society's vessel, RV OCEANIC, equipped with side scan sonar, located the wreck soon after. It was however, unable to relocate it again on subsequent tries. According to the manufacturer, the $17,000 boat with its lead keel and fiberglass-over-balsa construction, should have continued "sailing upright," skipping over the bottom and coming to rest somewhere deeper in the Sound.

TUG CONDOR
Chart #12363   Loran: 26831.7 (8-9) 43984.8(9)

On the evening of December 7, 1983, the 62-foot tug Condor, based at Bridgeport, Connecticut, was battling 5 foot seas off the Norwalk Islands. Earlier that day, gale winds had been recorded up to 54 mph. By evening however, the winds had slowed to 25 mph. At approximately 9:30 p.m., an electrical fire started aboard the 54-ton, 77-year-old vessel and a distress signal was sent out. The tug sank quickly; Captain Michael Desmond and his mate, Francis Scarano, were rescued from their life raft by a Coast Guard helicopter.

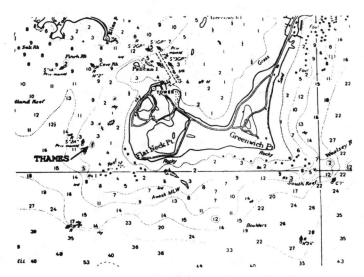

Greenwich Point: Thames (Sugar Boat)

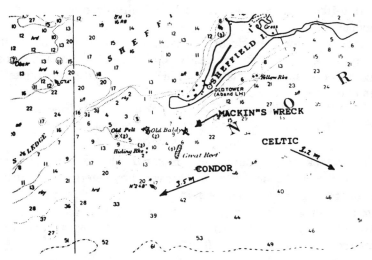

Sheffield Island: Celtic, Condor and Mackin's wreck

41

A preliminary report by the Marine Investigation Office of the Coast Guard indicated that the tug might have been engaged in unlawful activities, that is, smuggling of controlled substances. Norwalk Marine Police Officer, Bruce Mackin, the first diver to enter the wreck, found no evidence of illegal activities, nor did the Coast Guard.

The wreck lies on the bottom with its stern firmly implanted into the silt. Though all of its portholes have been removed, there is still plenty for a salvage diver to find. Visibility is usually poor due to the soft silt on which the wreck sits. Despite its size, the Condor is difficult to "hook." Should a diver anchor off the wreck, the vessel could be missed entirely in the low visibility water.

GREENS LEDGE LIGHT
Chart #12368 (Rowayton, Ct.)

Built in 1902 to replace Sheffield Island Light, Greens Ledge Light stands due south of the Five Mile River, in Rowayton, Connecticut.

Marine animals at the light consists of the usual variety, including coral, frilled anemones, sea stars, sea urchins and tube worms. Countless flounder, eel, toadfish, blackfish and cunner inhabit the site. At night, Greens Ledge is a popular spot for lobstering. The large boulders surrounding the lighthouse, form cathedral-like chambers which are beautifully decorated by frilled anemones.

Anchor on the lee side of the light, as close as possible to the lighthouse rocks. Currents can easily be managed by remaining close to the rocks. If anchored out too far, difficulty could be encountered when returning to the boat in a strong current.

MACKIN'S WRECK   Source: Bruce Mackin
Chart #12363, 12368 (Sheffield Is., Ct.)   Norwalk P.D.
Loran 43998.3(5) 26807.4(6) 15264.6 60039.0

The wreck of an unidentified, motorized barge lies inside the Great Reef near Sheffield Island. Discovered by veteran diver, Bruce Mackin, the prop and shaft are intact, while other structures are scattered over a wide area. The prop stands 7 to 8 feet tall and is completely covered with marine organisms including sponge, tube worms, coral and moss animals (bryozoans).

Approach to the wreck is hazardous. It is wise to visit the site at low tide and return for a slack high or low tide. Currents can be strong over the site. Depth probably does not exceed 20 feet.

AT EASE
Chart #12363

Source: Bruce Mackin
Norwalk P.D.

On July 11, 1951, a couple entered Norwalk Harbor aboard the 28-foot steel hull, At Ease, bound for an evening meal at a dock-side restaurant. They had rented the boat for a much-delayed honeymoon cruise. Sometime during the evening, an argument ensued and ultimately, the couple parted. The wife left the restaurant and taking the boat, headed west out of the harbor. At the south end of Sheffield Island, the vessel was observed running aground at least twice. On each occasion, the woman managed to free the boat. Later that evening, the inhabitants of the island heard a woman's screams. On the following morning, the wife's body, along with debris from the boat, were found on the island's shore.

SHEFFIELD ISLAND - CT.
Chart #12368, 12363

The south shore of Sheffield Island, near the old lighthouse, is a great dive for those who like to recover anchors. The rocky reefs which extend west from the end of the island, are a good hunting ground for lobster, blackfish and flounder. Current is *strong* over the site, thus it is best to dive at slack tide. Sailboats, moving silently over the reef, present the greatest hazard to divers. Always display a dive flag and, as much as possible, enter and exit by your boat.

CELTIC - CAPE RACE
Chart #12363   Loran: 26798.8(9) 43989.9(8)

The 84.8-foot tug Celtic was built in 1958 by Jakobson Shipyard of Oyster Bay, Long Island. Its first owner, Newtown Creek Towing, operated the tug as the Russell #10 until it was sold to McAllister Brothers and renamed, Judith McAllister. McAllister then sold it in February, 1981 to Ekloff Marine Corporation of Staten Island who changed the tug's name to Celtic. Under Ekloff, it operated on Long Island Sound, the Hudson River, the Connecticut River and along the coast from Delaware to Maine. On the evening of November 17, 1984, the Celtic was pushing the 150-foot barge, Cape Race, loaded with scrap metal. Fighting 3 to 5 foot seas as it

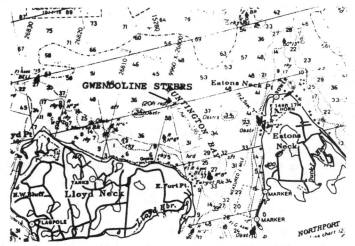

Eatons Neck-Target Rock: Gwendoline Steers

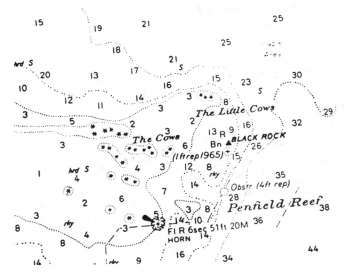

Penfield Reef Light

44

traveled from Bridgeport to Port Newark, New Jersey, the barge suddenly filled with water. Before the captain and crew could react, the Cape Race pulled the Celtic to the bottom, trapping the entire crew of six. (The Herbert E. Smith, a sister barge, also loaded with scrap metal, sank on the next day at Bridgeport Harbor pier.)

Officer Bruce Mackin of the Norwalk Marine Police, having the grim task of searching for and recovering the crew's bodies, was the first to dive the Celtic. The tug was found sitting upright on a hard surface, with the Cape Race just forward of her. Located in 60 feet of water, 1.5 miles south of Sheffield Island, (buoy WR-28) the wreck has become western Sound's most popular dive site. Current can be very strong over the wreck, thus it should be dived only at slack tide. Visibility varies between 1 to 15 feet.

CABLE AND ANCHOR REEF
Chart #12363 Buoy R24C

Located in mid-Sound off Eatons Neck, Cable and Anchor reef rises from 90+ feet to a depth of less than 25 feet. The bottom is covered with a variety of different size boulders. Many of the rocks are pock-marked with colonies of cold water coral, resembling small cotton balls. Depending upon the time of year, clumps of eyed sponge stand 2 to 10 inches tall. Cunner and blackfish are permanent residents, with toadfish occupying the underside of many of the larger stones. Lobstering can be good at the site.

Hazards include current and boat traffic. Anchor as close as possible to the buoy and dive only at slack tide. Entering and exiting on the anchor line will help avoid boat traffic, and keep you out of trouble with the current.

OLD SCOW
Chart #12363   Loran: 26799.2(1) 43983.8(7)

There is always a thrill when you know that you are probably the first to find and dive a wreck. However, had this one been treasure hunter Mel Fisher's first find, he, no doubt, would have quit then and there. The scow, which probably transported gravel, lies on the bottom at about a 30° angle in 70 feet of water, and rising to 52 feet. It is about 150 feet long and is mostly of

wood construction. Parts of its bulkheads and deck have given way, making entry easy. Most of its cleats and other hardware are still on her. If you dive the "Old Scow," be sure to go to the bottom and look around its keel for lobster. Watch for commercial boat traffic, and dive here only at slack tide.

GWENDOLINE STEERS

Source(s): Craig Steinmetz

Chart #12363,12365 (Huntington Bay, N.Y.) Ronnie Carl

Loran: 43951.4 26798.6

On December 30, 1962, the 87-foot tug Gwendoline Steers was proceeding toward Northport, New York, in near blizzard conditions. One week before, the 74 year old vessel had run aground near Greenwich, Connecticut. Entering Huntington Bay, the steel vessel suddenly took on water. It sank almost immediately, taking with it its captain, Herbert Dickman, and eight crewmen. One of the crew was able to escape aboard a lifeboat, only to die of exposure before reaching safety. Investigators found no apparent cause for the mishap, though one theory suggest heavy icing of the bow. Accusations were also made concerning improper maintenance by the tug's owners, Steers Sand and Gravel.

The largely intact wreck lies upright in 55 feet of water, rising 27 feet off the bottom. Visibility is generally poor, varying from 2 to 10+ feet. All of the portholes, gauges and other usually sought after souvenirs have been removed. Karls Mariners Inn, in Northport Harbor, has numerous artifacts on display which were recovered by the restaurant's owner and diver, Ronnie Carl.

TARGET ROCK

Chart #12363, 12365 (Huntington Bay, N.Y.)

Arriving by boat, run a course west of bell buoy R-8 in a direct line with Target Rock, a large boulder on the shore. Anchor about 600 to 800 feet offshore in 10 to 15 feet of water. The area is particularly interesting because of the large number of rocks, many of which are variously covered with sponge, coral, anemones and seaweed. The entire area is alive with blackfish, cunner, rock eel and flounder. Lobsters are found under many rocks and clumps of sulphur sponge. "Bugs," making their dens under sponge, are easy to retrieve since the sponge in underminded without difficulty.

Visibility is quite variable, from 2 to 10+ feet. Avoid diving here after heavy rains or during strong wave activity since visibility will then be at its worst.

EATONS NECK
Chart #12363, 12365 (Northport, N.Y.)

Unless you are in the Coast Guard or one of their dependents, the only access to diving Eatons Neck is by boat. The lighthouse which stands on a promontory, 100 feet above the water, is essentially the same structure that was first built in 1799.

Near shore, in 10 to 15 feet of water, the sea floor has large boulders that are often at a fair distance from each other. The bottom is a coarse sand in which occurs a phenomenon not seen as consistently in any other area of the Sound. Lying on the bottom, a diver can spook small fish called sandlaunce. Hiding in the sand the fish "fly" out of the bottom by the hundreds. The sandlaunce is so fast that even the 1/1000 second exposure of a flash is insufficient to capture it on film. Blackfish, cunner, flatfish and searobin also make their homes here. Lobster is common only farther offshore in deeper water.

Visibility varies from 5 to 15 feet and is influenced here mostly by wind direction. Current is a major hazard, necessitating diving only at slack tide.

EATONS NECK-BUOYS RB & 11B   Source: Al Neilson
Chart #12363, 12365   (Northport, N.Y.)

This is a good site for lobster, striped bass and blackfish. The bottom is lined with large boulders in depths of 35 to 70+ feet. Six wrecks of an unknown vintage have been reported (though unconfirmed) in very deep water, north of buoy 11B.

SMITHTOWN BAY - NORTHWEST CORNER
Chart #12363, 12365 (Northport, N.Y.)

Just around the point from Eatons Neck, the bottom is covered with small rocks on which grow seaweed, sponge and coral. Access is by boat, anchoring about 400 feet from shore.

The site is home for a large population of spider crab, flounder, rock eel, small lobster and occasional blue crab. During the day, divers, swimming over expanses of sand, will see small pairs of eyes peering up at them from the bottom. Closer inspection will reveal the large hermit crab, *Pagurus pollicaris,* that backs itself into the sand, giving it added protection from predators. (The shell that it occupies gives it its first line of defense). Nearer the rocks, a curious flatfish will often swim up to the human intruder and nip at an extended finger. Rolling over small rocks near the shore, will generally frighten a rock eel out of hiding. The underside of these same rocks also harbor a variety of other marine animals, including tube worms and tiny transparent ghost anemones.

Visibility ranges from 8 to 10+ feet. Watch for current during ebb and flood tides.

PECKS LEDGE LIGHT - Norwalk, Ct.

Chart #12363, 12368

There are some lobster around the base of the lighthouse rocks. Current is very strong as the tide falls or rises, with visibility never too good. Fishing lines are also a hazard at the light.

COCKENOE ISLAND REEF - COVE & SHOAL

Chart #12363, 12368 (Westport, Ct.)

Cockenoe Reef extends approximately 1000 yards out from the island's shore. Near the beach, the rocks are awash at low tide. The reef is difficult to find when covered with water. Thus, visit the site at low tide to orient yourself, and return for high slack tide, the best time to dive the reef.Marine life is plentiful on the reef, with larger lobster found at the outermost point of the reef. Blackfish, cunner and flounder are abundant. Pipefish, a relative of the seahorse, are found close to shore. Power and sailboat traffic are a serious hazard of this area. Be sure to trail a dive marker and use caution when surfacing.

The area near the entrance to the cove at Cockenoe Island, is popular for clamming. At low tide, there is no need for SCUBA gear. Some however, manage to dive the 3 to 4 foot depth in search of hard shell clams. (Get a permit from Westport Town Hall)

Cockenoe Shoal, on the south side of the island, runs in a N-S direction, away from the island. The only sure way to find it is with a depth sounder. The bottom is strewn with rocks of various sizes. Early summer lobstering is usually best. A number of wrecks have occurred on the shoal, though artifacts are difficult to find.

THOMAS TOMLINSON   Source: AWOIS-1984

Chart #12363   Lat/Long 41/00/00 73/20/00   NOAA

The 422-ton barge sank somewhere between Westport and Eatons Neck on August 3, 1942.

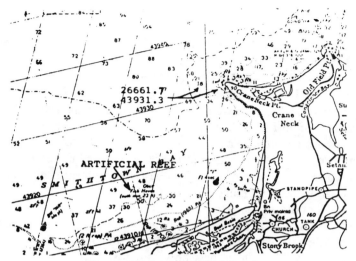

Crane Neck - Artificial Reef

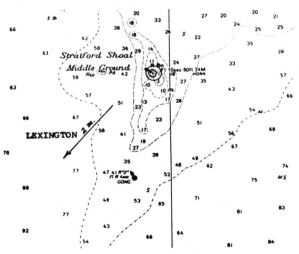

Stratford Shoal: Lexington

UNKNOWN WRECK

Source: AWOIS-1984

Chart #12363 Lat/Long 41/05/00 73/16/17 NOAA

Off Fairfield, Connecticut.

SMALL BARGE

Source: Bruce Makin

Chart #12363

Norwalk P.D.

Loran: 26747.9 43983.0

Found by Bruce Makin, the barge is located south of George's Rock, in about 66 feet of water.

SHERWOOD ISLAND STATE PARK

Chart #12363, 12368 (Westport, Ct.)

Sherwood Island, exit 18 on I-95, is one of the area's few dive sites accessible by land. After entering the gate, take the first right into a parking area, leaving you car at the far end of the lot. The designated area for diving is at the jetty, west of the stone pavilion (quite a hike for most divers). The best spot unfortunately, has been ruled out by the chief ranger.

The bottom at the jetty is mostly silt and fine sand, with some rocks. There are a few fish with a multitude of crabs scurrying about. Along the shore, divers occasionally find a mantis shrimp out of its burrow. The site is best however, for divers that just want to get their "fins wet," for family outings or for students going through training exercises.

Sherwood point, opposite to the park pavilion, is far more interesting, but accessible only by water. The rock reef extends about 500 feet from the beach and houses toadfish, lobster, blackfish, flounder and skate. The area's chief hazard is fishing gear. On a summer weekend, hordes of fishermen try their luck from the shore, at the point.

GLEN ISLAND: Courtesty–Mariners Museum, Newport News, Va.

Shaft structure, Mackin's Wreck (available light)

**LEXINGTON: Courtesy–Mariners Museum,
Newport News, Va.**

**LARCHMONT: COURTESY–Mariners Museum,
Newport News, Va.**

ONONDAGA: Courtesy–Peabody Museum of Salem

RHODE ISLAND: Courtesy–Peabody Museum of Salem

PENFIELD REEF LIGHT

Source Noel Voroba
Orbit Marine

Chart #12363, 12368 (Fairfield, Ct.)

Built in 1884, Penfield Reef Light has been witness to numerous boating mishaps, especially on the reef, "The Cows," just north of the lighthouse. Legend tells of smuggling and other strange happenings on the reef. The lighthouse itself is reputed to have once been haunted.

The man-made stone reef on which the lighthouse stands, is one of the most frequently dived spots in the western Sound. With a maximum depth of about 20 feet, the dive is good for beginners, though experienced divers will also enjoy it. Approach to the lighthouse should be made from the south or east, avoiding the reef on the northwest. A boater can easily anchor 30 to 50 feet from the rocks, preferably on the lee side.

The bottom near the light is covered with small rocks, sand and silt. The boulders supporting the facility are host to anemones that are an especially spectacular sight at night. Cold water coral, red beard, yellow and eyed sponge, abound. Lobster is common under rocks, with blackfish, cunner, flatfish, grubby and tomcod occupying each its own niche, in the vicinity. Though heavily dived, lobster is often caught at the light. Anchors and assorted fishing gear are normal finds for salvage divers.

Underwater debris, such as pipes and fishing lines are hazards to be watched for. Current does not present much of a problem provided that the diver stays near the lighthouse rocks. Visibility is best at high slack tide, in calm seas, after a period of little rain. At low tide, in choppy seas, water clarity can be miserable.

The pipe tower, slightly northeast of the light, is a good alternative dive site. Large boulder that are covered with seaweed, anemones, coral and sponge, line the bottom. The area is very good for lobstering in early summer. Current can be strong, thus it is best to dive during a slack time.

Parts of what may have been a barge are reported in the middle of the channel, off the jetty at Jennings Beach.

BRIDGEPORT BREAKWALL - Ct.

Chart #12363, 12369

The south side of Bridgeport Breakwall, at the end of Long Beach, is sometimes visited by area divers. The site offers a few lobster and loads of fishing gear. Visibility ranges from nihil to 5+ feet. The breakwall can be dived from shore before and after beach season. At other times, access is by boat only.

ARTIFICIAL REEF

Source: Craig Steinmetz
Jim Watson

Chart #12363   Smithtown Bay, N.Y.
Loran: 43915.7 26668.4 15186.1

Largely through the efforts of marine biologist, Steve Resler of the Department of Environmental Analysis, Stony Brook, an artificial reef was created off Long Beach Town Park. A number of steel cylinders, along with 20,000 tires, were sunk at the site. In 1981, a 348-foot railroad freight barge was scuttled on the same spot. The barge had originally sunk near the Bronx. Refloated, it was towed to the area. The wreck, broken in two parts, rests in 40 feet of water. The debris and barge are home for a profuse number of marine animals. Because of heavy diving pressure, lobstering is only good in early summer.

CRANE NECK POINT

Chart #12363, 12354 (Smithtown Bay, N.Y.)
Loran: 26661.7 43931.3

Crane Neck Point is consistently one of the more interesting dives in the western Sound. Rich in marine life, the site can only be reached by boat. One the southwest side of the point, steer the boat directly toward shore, aligning yourself with a very large 40 to 50 foot high boulder on the beach. The boat can safely be anchored 600 to 1000 feet offshore, in 10 to 25 feet of water. *The site should be dived only at low slack tide* since there is a dangerous current which develops soon after maximum high tide.

Close to shore, in 5 to 10 feet of water, rocks and boulders are covered with kelp, sargassum and other species of seaweed. In mid-June, a diver entering the water at this depth is greeted by a chorus of froglike sounds produced by mating male toadfish. At the height of its mating season, the ugly looking fish is found under and around, nearly every large rock. Later in the summer, pipefish and an occasional seahorse are found hiding among the weeds. Under some rocks is found an unusual mollusc, the chiton. Purple seas urchins, wedged between the rocks, are scattered throughout the area.

Farther from shore, in 20+ feet of water, the surfaces of the rocks are dotted with frilled anemones. Lobster can be found under rocks and clumps of yellow sulphur sponge. In the spring and early summer, rocks are sometimes completely covered with the pink flowerlike hydroids, *Tubularia crocea*. If a diver looks very carefully, the red or orange shell-less snail, nudibranch, can be seen grazing on hydroids. The pretty red blood starfish, seldom seen at the western end of the Sound, can also be found at the site.

Crane Neck abounds with cunner, blackfish, and flatfish including occasional searobin, skate, roughtail stingray and dogfish. Late July and August overgrowth of kelp can obscure much of the marine life. Average visibility ranges from a little less than 10 feet to 20+ feet. Onshore winds or rain can, however, reduce water clarity to 2 to 5 feet.

Around the other side of Crane Neck Point, toward the eastern end of the Sound, diving often is disappointing. Marine life is not nearly as lush, though lobstering can be good. It is, however, a good alternative when wind direction makes diving poor at the other side.

UNKNOWN WRECK   Source: AWOIS-1984
Chart #12363 Lat/Long 41/05/04.10   73/16/08.10   NOAA
    Off Smithtown Bay.

LEXINGTON   Source(s): Richard Taracka
Chart #12363, 12354, 12369   Bruce Mackin
Loran: 26652.1(2) 43962.8

Built in 1835, the Lexington was first owned by Cornelius Vanderbilt, who later sold the 205-foot sidewheel steamer to the New Jersey Steam Navigation and Transportation Company. On the night of January 13, 1840, the steamer was making its way along its usual route, from New York to Stonington, Connecticut. Just east of Eatons Neck, fire was discovered below decks. Fed by a cargo of cotton bales, the Lexington soon became a blazing inferno. At the inquest, it was learned that the new owners had converted the wood heated boiler to coal, adding a blower. It was felt that the intense heat generated, without adequate protection, might have started the fire. Fire then spread to the promenade deck via the intense heat in the smoke stack, or from sparks in the space between the smoke stack and the steam chimney.

As soon as fire was discovered, the captain headed for shore. The first lifeboat was launched with the steamer still under-way. It was immediately chewn-up by the paddlewheel. A second lifeboat set off into the night, overloaded, never to be seen again. The vessel soon lost power and streering, then drifted ablaze past Crane Neck Point. Estimates of up to 150 people perished that night; four survived by clinging to bales of cotton.

The Lexington was raised in 1842 only to break up and slide back to its watery grave. Some of its approximately $20,000 in silver was recovered, yet most of it remains on or near the steamer. A large portion of what might have been its bow, lies in 125+ feet of water, near Middle Ground. At that depth in Long Island Sound, *all is black* ! Visibility however, sometimes extends to the distance cast by the beam of a diver's light, 4 to 10 beet. A tether line is a *must,* if a diver has any hope of relocating the anchor line. Be sure to watch the dive tables and dive the wreck at slack tide.

OLD FIELD POINT - Port Jefferson, N.Y.
Chart #12354, 12362

The stone lighthouse marking Old Field Point was built in 1823. Replaced by a black skeleton tower in 1933, the old structure is maintained by the village of Old Field. Though the site can be reached by auto, the village fathers have an ordinance preventing diving from shore. Thus, the only access is by boat.

Beginning in early June, the underside of many of the large boulders are home for the mating toadfish. Sea robin, skate, flatfish, blackfish and cunner are plentiful, with an occasional pelagic or open water species, such as the roughtail stingray, visiting the area in late summer. Because of the abundance of suitable shelter, lobstering is generally good.

The area must be approached with caution. A number of rocks are awash at low tide, while others are lurking just below the surface. Anchor a little west of the lighthouse, about 700 feet offshore, in 15 to 20 feet of water. Since current can be very strong at the point, plan to dive here only at slack tide. Visibility ranges from 5 to 15+ feet.

MOUNT MISERY SHOAL   Source Bruce Coulter
Chart #12362 (Port Jefferson, N.Y.)   Port Diver SCUBA

Mount Misery Shoal lies about 3/4 mile off Port Jefferson

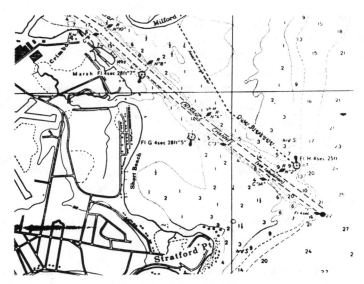

Stratford breakwall

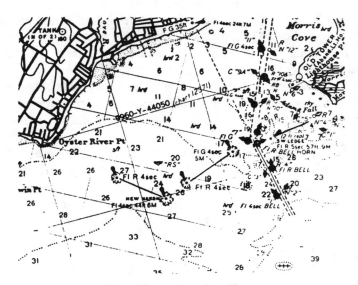

New Haven breakwall

58

Harbor. The outer limits of the dive site is marked by buoy C-11. Steering the boat shoreward from the buoy on a compass heading of between 220° to 230°, will make it easier to locate.

The bottom on the shoal is covered with different size rocks, making it one of the area's best dives. Large blackfish, cunner and sea robin have established residence on the shoal. Lobstering however, is one of the spot's main attractions.

Current can exceed 1 knot in velocity at the shoal, thus diving should be limited to slack tide. Visibility, often good, varies between 5 to 15+ feet.

SCHOONER MYRONUS   Source: AWOIS-1984
Chart #12354, 12362 Lat/Long 41/00/39.70 72/58/23.50

In the Early morning fog of August 12, 1907, the steamer Tennessee, bound for New York, collided with the schooner Myronus, east of Stratford Shoal. Nearly cut in two, the 118-foot, three masted schooner sank almost immediately, taking with it four of its crew. The Tennessee suffered little damage and its 350 passengers, though thrown into a state of panic, were not harmed.

Though not positively confirmed as the Myronus, remnants of a schooner rest approximately 7 nautical miles east of Stratford Shoal, in over 60 feet of water. (see area chart) The wreck consists of ribs and large timbers, the surfaces of which are mostly covered with anemones and hydroids. Visibility varies from nil to 10+ feet. Be sure to use a tether line.

STRATFORD SHOAL - MIDDLE GROUND
Chart #12363, 12354, 12369   Source: Noel Voroba
Orbit Marine

When Adrian Block sailed past Stratford Shoal in 1614, he charted two islands on the spot where the lighthouse now stands. The islands have since "washed away" and the over 100 year old light warns mariners of the nearby shoals.

Anchoring near the lighthouse, divers will find a wide variety of sea life. Coral, anemones, algae and sponge decorate the rocks. Flatfish, blackfish and cunner are normal residents while striped bass and bluefish are frequently seen. The remains on an unidentified wreck lies on the slope, west of the light. The usual finds for salvage divers however, are anchors and fishing gear.

Hazards include boat traffic and current. If a current is encountered, stay close to the lighthouse rocks. Its strength will be the greatest when rounding corners, though overall it can be managed by "walking" hand over hand on the bottom.

Taking advantage of the surface currents, dive shop owner Noel Voroba, sometimes takes his advanced students for a drift dive at the site. Hanging from a line attached to the boat, the divers are treated to a ride of up to 1.5 knots. A diver considering this type of dive should first be sure to get a reliable person piloting the boat.

STRATFORD BREAKWALL - Ct.
Chart #12354, 12370

The east side of Stratford Breakwall is a favorite with many area sport divers. The spot which can only be reached by boat, harbors toadfish, blackfish, cunner and lobster.

Current on the east side of the breakwall is generally no problem, however, the west side bordering on the Housatonic River can be deadly. A diver entering the water on the west side of the breakwall, at the height of a falling tide, will be in for a quick ride to mid-Sound. Visibility is best at high slack tide, in calm seas.

ANCHOR BEACH - Woodmont, Ct.
Chart #12354

The dive site is one of the few accessible spots from land at that end of the Sound. The rocks which are approximately 300 feet from the shore, harbor small lobster, toadfish, grubby, blackfish, flatfish and schools of cunner. Coral is found on rock surfaces in as little as 3 feet of water. By late August, the bottom, near the rocks, is carpeted with red beard sponge. The expanse between the offshore rocks and beach is mostly sand. Millions of small hermit crabs scurry about with an occasional skate seen in early summer. As with any area, the population of marine animals vary from year to year. Overgrowth of kelp also often hides other marine life. Thus, a site can be great on one dive (or one year) and poor the next. Visibility can be miserable at Anchor Beach if dived at low tide, after heavy rain and/or rough seas. A high tide with calm seas provides the best water clarity.

Directions: I-95, exit 41 Hill Rd., right turn on Merwin Ave., left on Chapel St., right on Kings Hwy. Parking near the beach is difficult in season.

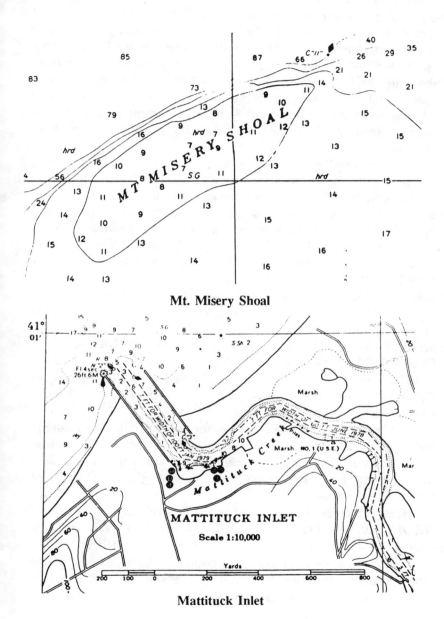

Mt. Misery Shoal

MATTITUCK INLET

Scale 1:10,000

Yards

Mattituck Inlet

61

NEW HAVEN BREAKWATER - Ct.
Chart #12354, 12371

The breakwater at the entrance of New haven Harbor is divided into three sections, one of which is at 90° to the other two. The nearly two nautical miles of breakwall can most always be dived on a "protected" side, away from wave action. Accessible only by boat, the wall can be approached quite closely, since the bottom drops sharply to 20 feet, sloping to about 40 feet.

The rocks on the breakwall form large caverns with anemones clinging to their inner surfaces. Sea stars grasp the rocks, with patches of coral weaved amongst growth of yellow sulphur sponge. In the spring and early summer, pink hydroids, *Tubularia crocea*, cover many of the rocks. The rocks also provide lobster with plenty of hiding places. The crustacean can easily be removed from its den at this site, by digging the loose sand out from under it. Cunner and large blackfish are usually found peering out from the rock crevices.

Visibility ranges from nil to 10+ feet. It is best at high slack tide in calm seas. The greatest hazard are the lobster pot lines.

CABIN CRUISER   Source: AWOIS-1984
Chart #12354, 12371   Lat/Long 41/12/17.26 72/55/41.28

A 20-foot cabin cruiser is reported in 31 feet of water, off New Haven Harbor.

MOUNT SINAI HARBOR - N.Y.   Source(s): Al Nielson
Chart #12354, 12362, 12364   Chuck McCormick

The jetties at Mount Sinai can be reached via land by driving to Cedar Beach, or by boat. Parking however, is allowed only for area residents during the summer season.

The jetties are a great spot for lobster and crab. Blackfish, cunner and flatfish are the most common fish at the site. Squid is encountered in late spring. The bottom at the harbor inlet is excellent for clamming. Large lobster and fluke make their home in a pile of debris, near the mid-inlet.

Hazards include heavy boat traffic and current.

WADING RIVER POWER PLANT   Source: Barbara Coulter
Chart #12354   Port Diver SCUBA Ctr

The Wading River Power Plant is about 13.5 miles east of the entrance to Port Jefferson Harbor. The dive site which is noted on the charts as "outfall," is marked by two privately maintained buoys.

Reaching out directly in front of the plant, depth over the outfall pipe ranges from 20 to 60 feet. The entire length of the rock covered pipe is great for lobster. Sponge and anemones cling to the sides of many of the rocks. The bottom near the shore end of the outfall is coarse sand and small rocks. Flats and other bottom fish are usually seen in this area.

Current is not ordinarily a problem at the Wading River site. Visibility varies from 5 to 15 feet.

THIMBLE ISLANDS - SCHOONER TRAVELER
Chart #12354, 12373 (Stony Creek, Ct.)

On August 12, 1907, the two masted schooner Traveler, loaded with 250 tons of brownstone bound for New York markets, ran aground and broke up inside Brown's Reef. It was probably one of many shipwrecks that dot the Thimble Islands' shores. The Islands are rich in local legend including a story of Captain Kidd who buried gold on Money Island. However, had the famous pirate hidden his loot at all of the sites that claim such a history, he would have spent most of his time digging! Though it would be nice to retire on the scoundrel's treasure, that is probably best left to dreamers.

Extending to a mile off the mainland, the Islands are accessible only by boat. The sea floor is mostly silt and mud, with many areas of rock reefs. The reefs are the best bet for lobster and for spearing blackfish. Flatfish are found on the mud/silt bottom. The rocks themselves are variously covered with anemones, coral, starfish, sponge, barnacles and seaweeds. Visibility averages less than 5 feet.

WOODEN DRYDOCK   Source: AWOIS-1984
Chart #1235   Lat/Long 41/09/21.58 72/44/58.01   NOAA

A wooden drydock rests in 90+ feet of water, about 6 miles southeast of the Thimble Islands. Entry into the relatively intact structure is easy,. as some of its bulkheads have given way. Visibility is usually poor, varying from 3 to 10 feet.

FALKNER ISLAND - Guilford, Ct.
Chart #12354, 12373

Rising from the water like a surfacing submarine, Falkner Island stands about 3 miles off Guilford, Connecticut. Arriving via boat, anchor near the old lighthouse dock. The rocks in the area are alive with hundreds of schooling cunner. Seaweed and sponge cover nearly every available space, with some blood starfish clinging to the underside of rocks. The large hermit crab, *Pagarus pollicaris,* is frequently seen dragging its huge home, a welk or moon snail shell. Small lobster inhabit the rocks near the dock; the larger, "legal sized" lobster is usually in deeper water. There is not much excitement here for the die-hard salvage diver. Bruce Berman (Encyclopedia of Shipwrecks) does, however, list several wrecks in the vicinity,. any of which would be great to locate.

Strong current can be encountered at both the north and south ends of the island. Boating traffic is heavy on weekends, so be sure to trail a dive float. Depth ranges to about 20 feet, and visibility, dependent upon the prevailing weather conditions, varies between 5 to 15 feet.

UNIDENTIFIED AIRPLANE - Riverhead, N.Y.
Chart #12354 Loran: 43903.7 26450.1 60052.6

An unidentified aircraft lies approximately 1500 yards offshore in 30 to 40 feet of water, near Reeves Beach. A small section of the aircraft was pulled up when a commercial dragger got his nets caught in it. Though not dived by the author, the Loran fix on it is no doubt accurate, since it was obtained from the trawl-fisherman himself.

ROANOKE POINT - REEVES BEACH Source: Ron Zaleski
Chart #12354 (Riverhead, N.Y.)   7Z's Hampton Bay Divers

The two dive sites can easily be reached by auto. Roanoke Point, at the end of Roanoke Point Road, has numerous rocks near shore, a perfect spot for lobster. A short distance to the west, at Reeves Beach, lies a barge submerged in shallow water. The wreck is 100 to 150 yards offshore, about midway between the two barges on the beach. The beach can be reached by making a left hand turn just before Roanoke Point and a right to the water. A four-wheel-drive vehicle can then be driven down the beach to the site.

Small marine creatures have grown over the entire barge, making the structure a good spot for close-up photographers. Cunner and blackfish cruise over the barge, while flatfish and the large hermit crab share the area's sandy bottom. Lobster and crab that hide within the wreckage are easy pickings as they emerge for their nightly forays.

Current, usually not a problem, should still always be watched for. Visibility averages 5+ feet.

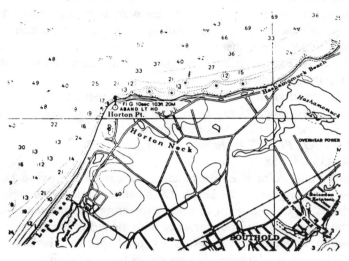

Horton Point

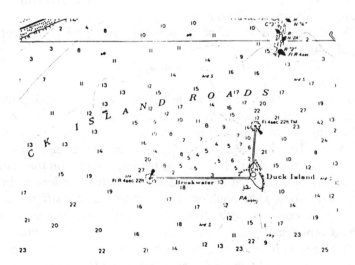

Duck Island breakwall

65

MATTITUCK INLET
Chart #12354, 12358

Source: Chuck McCormic
Swim King Dive Shop

The jetties at Mattituck Inlet are accessible by boat or auto. Both west and east jetties make a good dive site, though the east jetty is more luxuriant in sea life. American eel wind their way through the labyrinth of rocks. Blue crab, the pugnacious crustacean with especially sharp claws, shares the rocks with the other local delicacy, the lobster. Blackfish and cunner also reside there with flounder inhabiting the sandy bottom.

A shallow dive of 7 to 12 feet, it is best to visit the jetties at high tide. Visibility ranges from 0 to 15+ feet. Current can be a real problem on the *channel* sides of the jetties.

DUCK POND POINT - Mattituck, N.Y.
Chart #12354, 12358

Duck Pond Point is easily reached via car by following Depot Road to a parking lot on the beach. On an ebbing tide, walk west 1/4 mile up the beach to a point of rocks projecting out into the Sound. Enter the water and return underwater with the aid of the falling tide. The bottom, covered with rocks, is a natural spot for blackfish and lobster. The area is a favorite of many divers for night diving.

DUCK POND WRECK - (UNIDENTIFIED)
Chart #12354   Source: AWOIS-1984
Lat/Long: 41/06/45.44 72/32/10.92

AWOIS reported an unknown wreck in about 65 to 70 feet of water, off Duck Pond Point.

HORTON POINT LIGHT - Southhold, N. Y.
Chart # 12354, 12358

When George Washington visited Horton Point in 1750, prior to his presidency, he proposed the construction of a lighthouse on the site. As things go in Washington, it took only a little over 100 years to build it. The 1857 lighthouse looks over the Sound from its position on a promontory. Just east of the light, noted on the charts, are a few remains of what may have been a fishing or lobster boat. Nearby, a 20-foot wide boulder rises almost 12 feet off the sand bottom. It is covered with dime-sized anemones, hydroids, and numerous other marine animals competing for space. Hundreds of small fish seek shelter around the rock including cunner, sea robin and very large blackfish. Several other large boulders standing offshore, are of equal interest. All, however, are in the midst of *very strong* currents. As the tide falls, eddies form around the boulders, making them easy to spot from the surface. Nearer the shoreline, current is much weaker. A diver entering the water from a boat should consider using a tether line. It would facilitate returning to the boat in a strong current. One must also be cautious of jellyfish at the site. During the height of the jellyfish season, the creatures tend to get caught-up in the eddies, concentrating them.

The site is accessible by boat and land. Unfortunately, the stairs leading down the step bank from the lighthouse, are less than sturdy. A diver weighted down with all that equipment, could have a nasty accident.

INLET POINT - Greenport, N. Y.   Source: Scott Marschean
Chart #12354, 12358

Inlet Point has an easy access across the road from the KOA campground. The rock strewn bottom at the point drops almost immediately to a depth of 25 to 30 feet. Large patches of yellow sulphur sponge are dispersed over the sea floor. The sandy bottom makes it easy to retrieve lobster hiding beneath the rocks. Blackfish, cunner and winter flounder patrol the area, with striped and black bass visiting on occasion. Watch for longshore current at this site.

TUG BARATARIA   Source: AWOIS-1984
Chart #12354 Lat/Long: 41/10/29.5 72/25/34.4   NOAA

The tug Barataria, also known as the El Morro 11, was built in Beaumont, Texas, in 1937. For a time, the 68-foot steel vessel was used to tow scows along the southern New England coast. On September 21, 1971, the Kidd Construction Company sold the tug to the Sun Marine Company, who sailed it to Middletown, Connecticut for refitting. In the process, some of its bulkheads were removed. On November 25, 1971, the tug set out for Miami, Florida in a gale. Waves broke over the bow, causing the collapse of some of its bulkheads. The ship then quickly took on water, sending it to the bottom off Horton Point. Two of the crew, William Corres and Charles Walsh, were lost; the owner, Ted Tanos, and another crewman, survived. The wreck of what may be the Barataria, or that of the tug, Thames, or yet another tug which sank on December 9, 1939, lies in 136 feet of water, rising 8 feet off the bottom.

TUG THAMES   Source: AWOIS-1984
Chart #12354 Lat/Long: 41/09/19.25 72/25/04.09

During an autumn 1973 storm, the tug Thames, owned by International Underwater Contractors, was towing the barge #143, off Horton Point. The 55-foot long, 87-year-old wrought iron vessel began rolling, leaning over to a point that it took on water. The pumps immediately shorted out and despite the best efforts of the crew, it became apparent that the tug was about to sink. The crew then transferred to the barge, set an anchor, and called for the Coast Guard. It is believed by NOAA divers, that the tug which sits in 100+ feet off Horton Point, is the Thames.

KAREN E (yet to be located)   Source: USCG Report
Chart # 12354   16732/034586/JJS

In the early morning hours of August 10, 1981, the 35-foot cabin cruiser Karen E, had lost most of its electrical power and the starboard engine. Through a series of human errors by its captain, Richard Lubin, the vessel collided with a barge which was being towed by the tug, David McAllister. The accident occurred near buoy CF, off Rocky Point, New York. Five people, including the captain's wife and his 10 year old daughter, were lost on the ill-fated vessel. The captain survived by swimming to shore.

There were accusations by Lubin, of being run down by the tug, along with conflicting testimony on both sides. In order to help establish the cause of the accident, the Coast Guard mounted an extensive search for the Karen E. Despite the use of a side-scan sonar and the unmanned submersible submarine, SCARAB, owned by the American Telephone and Telegraph Co., the Karen E was never located. The search took place approximately 0.3 miles north of the CF buoy on a base course of 70°. Coordinates of the search area corners were as follows: SW corner 41/11/1N, 72/22/2W, SE corner 41/12/9N, 72/16/0W, NW corner 41/12/1N, 72/22/7W, NE corner 41/13/8, 72/16/5W. (Depths in this area ranges from 110 to 160+ feet)

Though Lubin was found at fault, civil penalty action was initiated against both parties, since the McAllister barge had been improperly lit at the time of the accident.

STEEL BARGE
Source: AWOIS-1984
Chart #13254 (?)   Lat/Long: 41/12/54 72/17/36   NOAA

A barge covered with marine growth, lies in 140 feet of water, west of Orient Point, N.Y.

WRECK - AT 128 FEET
Source: AWOIS-1984
Chart #13254 (?)   Lat/Long: 41/13/18.60 71/11/51

Unidentified wreck, located west of Orient Point.

TUG - JOHN A. DOWNS
Source: Cdr David H. Lyon
Chart #12354   Lat/Long: 41/14/09N 72/07/51W   USCG

The winter of 1984-1985 saw two tugs lost to the waters of Long Island Sound, The Celtic and John A. Downs. On March 3, 1985, the 113-foot Downs, owned by the Great Lakes Dredge and Dock Company of Staten Island, was towing three barges in 4 to 5 foot seas. Two miles northwest of Great Gull Island, at the extreme eastern end of Long Island Sound, the tug somehow collided with one of its barges, leaving an 8-foot hole in its side. Attempts to plug the hole with mattresses were of no avail. Captain Douglas Sible then gave the order to abandon ship, whereupon he and his crew of 8 boarded one of the barges. The John A. Downs now lies in 230 feet of water, beyond safe sport diving depth.

HAMMONASSET STATE PART - Madison, Ct.
Chart #12354, 12374

Hammonasset State Park, exit 62, on I-95, is the type of dive site that can be enjoyed by the whole family. Its beach, fishing, campgrounds and play areas can keep the non-divers busy while the divers do "their thing."

After paying an entry fee (higher on summer weekends), proceed to Meigs Point, the designated dive site at the park. Entry can be made anywhere east of the fishing jetty. The bottom is covered with rocks on which dwell small anemones, sponge, Christmas treelike bryozoans and various species of seaweed. Most lobster in the area are undersized. In addition to the usual cunner, blackfish and flatfish, late spring brings schooling squid in close to shore.

Visibility, never too good at Hammonasset, averages only 5+ feet. That is no doubt due to the silting from nearby Clinton Harbor. Current is weak near shore but "rips" farther out. Thus, it is best to stay near and parallel to shore. Depth ranges to about 17 feet.

DUCK ISLAND BREAKWALL - *Clinton, Ct.*
Chart #12354, 12374

The south side of the Duck Island breakwall, offers a shallow dive to lobstering sportsmen. On the reef south-east of the wall, wreckage of an unidentified wreck lies scattered over a large area. Unfortunately, it is nearly impossible to dive the site except for a very short time at slack tide.

The rocks at the breakwall are covered with the dime-sized anemones, commonly seen in the area. Cunner weave their way through the rocks with some flatfish inhabiting the sea floor. Visibility is often poor. The main hazards here are the numerous lobster pots whose lines could easily entangle a diver.

PLEASURE BEACH   Source: Gerry Lynn
Chart #12354, 13211 (Waterford, Ct.)

Pleasure Beach affords the diver easy access for a shore dive. Entry is made south of the boat launch ramp, avoiding the private property and beach areas on both sides of the ramp. Depth here is at a maximum of 15 feet, with most of the diving even shallower. The shoreline is bordered by eelgrass that harbors an active community of marine animals including occasional scallops. Cunner hover over the offshore rock areas with lobster, usually undersized, making their dens beneath the rocks. Spawning squid are encountered in late spring, a short distance offshore. Visibility averages 5 feet. The chief hazard at this site is boat traffic, making a divers flag even more important. The area is frequently patrolled by state (DEP) wardens, who are well known by local divers for their enforcement of the dive flag law.

A short distance from Pleasure Beach, Waterford Town Park is available during the beach season, to town residents only. The bottom is similar to that of Pleasure Beach.

HARKNESS MEMORIAL PARK & SEASIDE
REGIONAL CTR.
Chart #12354, 13211   Source(s) Gerry Lynn
(Waterford, Ct.)   Joe Berardy

Formerly an estate which was donated to the state' of Connecticut, Harkness Memorial Park includes the Seaside Regional Center. The area offers some of the best beach diving along the Connecticut shore. Beach entry is possible at two locations, the

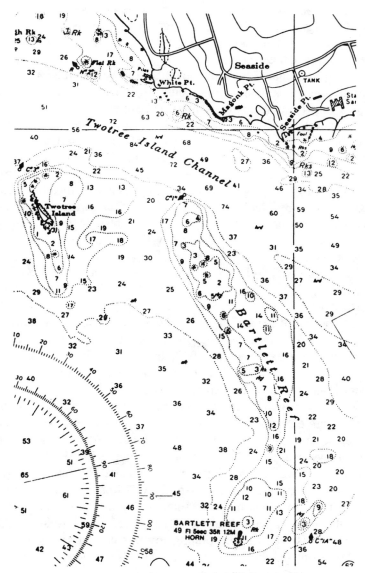

Twotree Island Channel-Bartlett Reef

71

public area and the Seaside Regional Center.

Enter the area at the public area (museum facility), after crossing a small stream which drains Goshen Cove; swim east toward the rocks near Goshen Point. The bottom is mostly sand with some rocks. Offshore, in 20 feet of water, boulders rise toward the surface. Cunner and blackfish reside among the rocks, with flatfish, lobster and crab at their base.

Seaside Regional Center is a facility for the mentally retarded. Before diving, check in at the main building where you may be asked to sign a log. (The structure is marked "State Sanatorium" on the nautical charts). The breakwater directly in front of the building, and the one just to the west, are interesting places to start to a dive. Lobster, cunner and blackfish inhabit the sites. Between the two, the sandy bottom is home for flounder and a few skate. Farther from shore, the bottom drops gradually, with rock outcroppings harboring a large number of blackfish. At Seaside Point (west of the two breakwalls), the sea floor drops rapidly to 60+ feet. As you go deeper in the Twotree Island Channel, visibility improves, while the shallows tend to average only 5 feet.

THE SUBMARINE, G-2

Chart #13254, 13211
(Waterford, Ct.)

Source: Bob Koller
Shoreline SCUBA

Construction of the G-2 by the Lake Torpedo Boat Company, of Bridgeport, Connecticut, was begun on October 20, 1909. The sub was launched on January 10, 1912, and before it could become commissioned on February 6, 1915, it had already become obsolete. The vessel was then used for experimental purposes.

The Navy began trials to determine how close they could detonate depth charges, without opening up the seams on the G-2. It was their intent to eventually sink the sub. At one point, the explosions warped the main hatch. It was removed and taken to the shipyard for repair. During that time, not realizing that seams had opened, some of the men went aboard the G-2 to blow out her ballast tank. Without warning, the sub suddenly went down stern first, striking the bottom with a tremendous force. Quartermaster C.E. Kirk worked his way to the conning tower hatch in shoulder deep water. As he opened the hatch, the outrushing air released him from a sure death. Three men died aboard the sub.

The G-2 was partially salvaged in 1962. What is left of the wreck lies in about 62 feet of water, in Twotree Island Channel, off Sea Side Park. Diver Bob Koller, describes the remants as somewhat resembling a rotting oil tank that has just been dug up. There is not much hope of recovering artifacts on the site. Current can be strong in the channel.

THE DEFENSE

Chart #12354, 13211 (Bartlett Reef - Waterford, Ct.)

Long Island Sound's "treasure ship" began its maritime career as the Lily Ann, a West Indies trader, whose home port was Greenwich, Connecticut. In December of 1775, the vessel was purchased from John Griggs of Greenwich. It then became part of Connecticut's young navy that would eventually grow to 14 ships. Renamed Defense, the vessel was sailed to New Haven for refitting, arming it with 20 swivel guns and 16 six-pounder cannons.

During the late fall of 1778, the Defense and other state navy ships were "bottled-up" in their harbors by an overwhelming British

fleet under the command of Admiral Arbuthnot. In the first week of March 1779, the captain of the Defense, Samuel Smedley, left the safety of New London Harbor, with his ship undermanned due to sickness. On a reconnoitering mission in

Long Island Sound, the ship found more than it had bargained for! Outgunned by several British warships, the Defense was driven back toward New London. Trying to reach the protective cover of the harbor's guns, the ship cut too close to shore and went aground on Goshen's Reef, now known as Bartlett Reef. The vessel immediately took on water, trapping four or more men below its decks. In a letter from Captain Smedley to Governor Trumbull dated March 12, 1779, the captain stated, "finding my situation such as there was no possibility to saving the ship, I immediately dispatched Captain Lloyd of the detachment to Mr. Shaw for lighters (barges) which were soon supplied. After about thirty hours fatigue, up to our middles in water, we secured all our guns, rigging, warlike stores, provisions and *everything of any value above water."* Much of the ship's armament was later transferred for use aboard the sloop Guilford.

There have been a number of published references to a treasure of silver and gold specie, brought on, in part, by the captain's statement, "..everything of any value above water." The Defense had been patrolling the Sound for only a short time in March of 1779, before coming to rest on the reef; so where did they strike it rich? (Could it have been a payroll, $500,000.?) With or without silver and gold however, finding the Defense would be a real treasure to any historians of the Revolutionary War period.

OCEAN BEACH - NEW LONDON, CT.
Chart #12354, 13212   Source: Ron Phillips

Located on the charts between Goshen Point and the clock tower, Ocean Beach is accessible by auto. After paying a parking fee, a diver must carry gear to the end of the boardwalk, across the beach, to a small stream at the entrance to Alewife's Cover. Enter the water at this point. There is a short swim to offshore rocks, called Shore Rock and Middle Rock.

The bottom surrounding the rock reef is sandy, with patches of eelgrass. The reef is home for scallop, blackfish, cunner, striped bass, lobster and blue crab. Clumps of blue mussel are attached to the rocks, with sponge and small anemones competing for living space. Maximum depth in the area is about 20 feet, with visibility averaging 10 feet. Current, which runs in an east-west direction, can be strong at times, attaining a flow of nearly 1.5 knots.

NEW LONDON LEDGE LIGHT
Chart #12354, 13212 (New London Harbor, Ct.)

On the east side of the entrance, New London Ledge Light provides good lobstering with blackfish, cunner and flatfish normal inhabitants of the spot. The rocks surrounding the lighthouse are dotted with the large frilled anemone. Though some divers have dived the light by swimming out to it, it is best to go by boat.

STEEL BARGE - New London   Source: AWOIS-1984
Chart #12354   Lat/Long: 41/15/24 72/05/00   NOAA

AWOIS reports a 90-foot long steel barge, near the dumping ground lighted buoy, off New London.

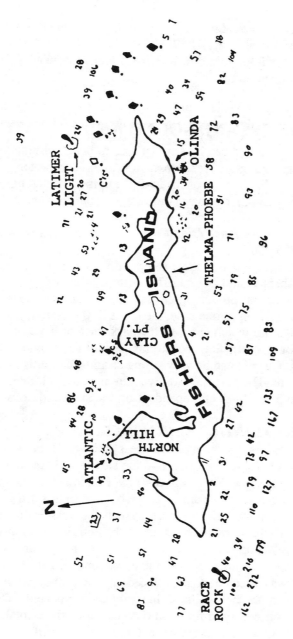

Fishers Island

LAZY DAYS - New London   Source: AWOIS-1984
Chart #12354 Lat/Long: 41/17/24 72/04/42   NOAA
A 36-foot fiberglass cruiser burned and sank near the mouth of New London Harbor.

FISHERS ISLAND SOUND AND VICINITY

Fishers Island Sound can be a tricky area to dive. Currents are *strong* during tidal changes, even close to shore. The waters, however, support a wide variety of beautiful marine life along with the potential of finding the remains of some very old shipwrecks.

NORTH HILL - Fisher Island   Source: Joe Berardy
Chart #13205, 13214

North Hill is rated by local veteran divers as one of the best dive sites in Fishers Island Sound. The bottom is crowded with 20-foot or larger boulders, producing caves that are natural shelters for the profuse marine life. In one case, the rocks have taken on the shape of a giant well from which emerges the dark form of blackfish. The site is great for spearfishing, lobstering, underwater photography or sightseeing. Current can be very strong at mid-tide but is manageable on the bottom. The best time to dive here is at a slack tide. Visibility varies from 5 to 20+ feet, dependent on the sea conditions and time of year.

STEAMER ATLANTIC - NORTH HILL

North Hill is the site of the best known of Fishers Island's shipwrecks. On November 26, 1846 the side-wheel steamer Atlantic, was bound for New York out of New London. Losing all power near Bartlett Reef, the steamer set anchor. Despite setting out even more anchors, storm-driven waves pushed the vessel all the way to North Hill. There, it went up on the rocks with its bow only 20 feet from shore. Within 15 minutes, the steamer had been reduced to floating timbers, with a considerable amount of loss of live. The ship's bell was recovered and placed at the top of what became locally known as Bell Hill; it has since disappeared. The ship's boilers were once easy to find, but time has done them in also. There is no doubt, however, that with a lot of effort, artifacts from the wreck can still be found.

PROBABLE WRECK
Source: AWOIS-1984

CHART #13214 Lat/Long: 41/16/26.50 72/02/38.80   NOAA

Appearing on the charts as clearing at 23 feet, AWOIS reports a probable wreck off North Hill.

CLAY POINT, BUOY C-5, Fishers Island
Chart 13214

Large rocks rising 8 to 10 feet off the sea floor, form canyons a short distance northeast from buoy C-5. The topography and varied marine life provide for an interesting dive. Current can be very strong all along the area, thus it should only be dived at slack tide.

Farther east, at buoy N-2E, the bottom is similar, though shallower than at C-5. Inside East Harbor, a marine railway runs offshore. Beams, cables assorted debris are scattered on the bottom. Old Bottles are sometimes found in the same vicinity.

RACE ROCK & WICOPESSET PASSAGE
Chart #13205, 13214   Source: Joe Berardy

Located on opposite ends of Fisher Island, Race Rock and Wicopesset Passage are for the *experienced divers only.* The currents, which can exceed 4 knots, are some of the strongest encountered in the entire area. They can, however, provide a thrilling drift dive as long as everything is well planned in advance. At Race Rock, large boulders, some of which were laid during the construction of the lighthouse, line the bottom. The dive should not be attempted during periods of low water visibility. Boating traffic, always heavy on summer weekends, is a major hazard at both sites.

SS OLINDA
Chart #12354, 13214 Loran: 26059.0 43966.7

The SS Olinda, sometimes mistaken for the steamer Vanderbilt, has been variously reported to have sunk on June 2, 1895 or June 11, 1895, on the south side of Fishers Island. Sailing too close to shore in a dense fog, the vessel ran up on the rocks off Goose Hammock. Its cargo of cork and empty barrels was saved, though the ship was a total loss. The bow, sticking out of the water, served for years as a reminder of the area's dangers. Approximately one year after the sinking, the steamer Tillie, with a cargo of sardines, ran aground in the same area. It was pulled free only to be lost at sea on a later trip.

The easy to find SS Olinda, lies in 30 feet of water, inside the bay marked on the charts, "Wreck Island." A long, cylindrical structure which may have been a mast, runs perpendicular to the beach. It is covered with barnacles, seaweed and small hydroids. Blackfish and cunner hover over the structure. The ship's boiler, the largest visible remains of the ship, is south of the mast. Totally encrusted with marine life, it houses small lobsters. The nearby rock reef is better for lobstering, though care must be taken with the surge produced by onshore waves. About 200 yards east of the boiler, other parts of the ship lie exposed in the sand.

Approach the wreck from the east with caution. The boiler is about 150 feet from the southeast end of the rock reef. Visibility averages between 10 to 25+ feet, being best in calm seas. Current is generally not a problem at the wreck.

THELMA-PHOEBE (Onward) & COLUMBIA
Chart #12354, 13214

On April 28, 1923, the yacht Thelma-Phoebe (also known as the Onward) lost it rudder and was driven up on the western end of Chocomount Beach, at the south side of Fishers Island. Part of its cargo of Scotch was "liberated" by local citizens before the Coast Guard could prevent it. Sometime thereafter, wreckers blew up the vessel.

Diving the area several times, this diver was able to locate only what appeared to be a mast, similar to that of the SS Olinda, but no well-aged Scotch!

In December of 1923, another vessel broke up and sank after running aground on the rocks at Barley Field Cove, next to Chocomount Beach. The 50 foot cabin cruiser, Columbia, had been smuggling whiskey

LATIMER REEF LIGHT and NORTH DUMPLING LIGHT
Chart #13214   Source: Joe Berardy
(Fishers Is. Sound—Mystic Ct.)

The rocks supporting Latimer Reef Light are an excellent hiding place for lobster. Blackfish and many other species also frequent the spot. At the opposite end of Fishers Island Sound, the island on which stands North Dumpling Light, is surrounded by a rock strewn bottom. The area provides lobster and very large clams along the

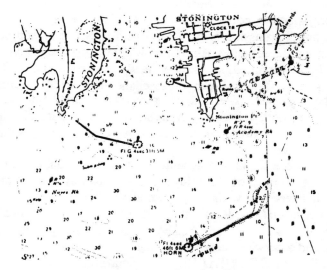

Stonington breakwall

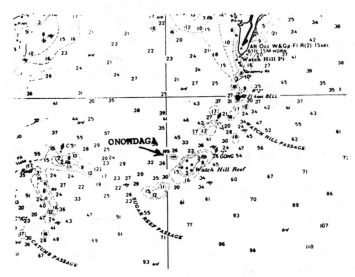

Watch Hill, wreck of the Onondaga

79

cable which runs from the island to its neighbor, South Dumpling. Several barges lie on the bottom, east of North Dumpling.

ENDERS ISLAND & RAM ISLAND   Source: Ron Phillips
Chart #13214   (Fishers Is. Sound—Mystic, Ct.)

Enders Island is connected to the mainland via a causeway to Mason Island. Permission to dive from its shores can sometimes be obtained from the religious retreat-house occupying the island. It is, however, less complicated to dive the island's shores by boat.

The island's shoreline can provide shelter from the wind, by diving the lee side. The sea floor is sandy and rock strewn. Lobstering is good, especially at night. Blue crab also inhabit the area. The rocks supporting the causeway, are overgrown by a variety of marine life forms.

Current which flows in a general east-west direction, can be very strong in the vicinity of the bridge at the causeway. Depth ranges from 5 to 15+ feet with visibility averaging 5 to 10+ feet.

The north end of Ram Island is great for clamming. The numerous shoals throughout Fishers Island Sound provide good lobstering and otherwise interesting diving.

STONINGTON BREAKWALLS   Source(s): Joe Berardy
Chart #13214   (Stonington, CT.)   Ron Phillips

The three breakwalls at the entrance of Stonington Harbor protect the area from storms. Access to the outer and west breakwalls is by boat; the inner wall is easily reached from the shore.

The west end of the outer breakwall is by far the most productive for lobster. Cunner, stripers, blackfish, and flounder frequent the site. The west breakwall is home for a large number of blackfish, cunner, American eel and lobster, with the pretty sea vase (a sea squirt) attached to the rocks. The animal has a transparent body and yellow trimmed openings to its siphons that close tightly under a divers light. From the parking lot at Stonington Point, a diver can swim to the inner breakwall, or simply dive the point. Old bottles are sometimes found along the shoreline, in an area north and adjacent to, the inner breakwall. Venturing out beyond the inner breakwall into the channel, however, can lead to an unplanned drift dive on a strong current, straight for mid-Fishers Island Sound. Be sure to trail a diver's float. The area is often visited by wardens only too willing to impose a fine for not diving with a flag.

(For the non-diving members of the family, or between dives, a visit to the nearby Stonington Lighthouse Museum is always worthwhile.)

COASTAL RHODE ISLAND

Rhode Island's waters are a mecca for southern New England and New York divers. They generally offer better visibility than many other area sites, but what especially makes the area attractive to out-of-staters, are the numerous beach access dive sites. Water clarity is often best in Rhode Island's offshore waters, during the late summer, as the Gulf Stream swings closer to the coast. There are times, however, that phytoplankton blooms (microscopic drifting plants), reduce visibility to less than five feet. Divers planning excursions to "open coastal sites," should watch for onshore wave action with heavy surf. It can severely reduce clarity and make the dive anything but a pleasure.

ONONDAGA   Source: Frank Johnson
Chart #13205, 13214 (300 yds west of buoy I)
Loran: 43966.6(2) 26026.3(5.7) 14628.0(7.6)60136.9

The Clyde Line freighter Onondaga, bound from Boston to Jacksonville, ran up on the reef at Watch Hill in a heavy fog, on June 28, 1918. The entire crew of 35 were saved. Built in 1905 at Philadelphia, the 2,696-ton freighter was loaded with a general cargo. Two months after the mishap, the George Hudson, a fishing steamer, struck the nearby reef and sank.

Bottles, china and shoe heels, inscribed "Cats Paw," are a common find on the wreck, which was reduced to a mass of twisted metal by wreckers' dynamite. Narrow-gauge tires of the era are found scattered around the wreck. Marine photographers will also find ample subjects. The frilled anemone, in a variety of colors, covers exposed surfaces of the boilers, plating and ribs. Near the bottom or under beams, marine life buffs will find the bright red anemone, *Telia*, which competes with any seen in the Caribbean. Both hard and soft coral inhabit the wreck. During the day, the soft coral looks like a finger(s), which has contributed to its common name, "dead man's finger." At night or in subdued light, the soft coral has a fuzzy appearance. The odd looking sea raven frequents the Onondaga, along with the usual cunner, tautog (blackfish) and eel. Lobstering is often quite good at the wreck.

CURRENT is the greatest hazard on the site. The Onondaga *must be dived at slack tide.* Entering the water 1/2 hour before slack will give a diver about one hour of bottom time, at the 50 foot depth. Visibility ranges from 10 to 40+ feet dependent on sea conditions and time of year. The best time to dive it for clarity, is in late August.

WATCH HILL REEFS

Chart #13214 (Rhode Island)

The reefs at Watch Hill have claimed numerous vessels including the US cutter Revenge (1811), the Brig. Adelnia (1815), the schooner Gulnare (1860), the schooner Cape May (1861), the schooner Eben Sawyer (1862), and the Laura Clinch (1864). Margaret Carter, in her book, "Shipwrecks on the Shores of Westerly," lists over 200 wrecks on or near Watch Hill reefs! With that kind of history, it surely is a good place to look for artifacts.

The only access to the reefs is by boat. It is probably best to visit the sites at least once at low tide, since many of the rocks are awash at that time. (Bring an extra prop!) Current is a real hazard at any of these reefs. Thus, be sure to dive only at slack tide and have someone stay on board the boat.

STEAMER LARCHMONT

Chart #13205   Loran: 43949.0(2)   25998.1(3)   14616.4(6)

Sailing from New York to Providence, Rhode Island, the steamer Larchmont entered the waters of Block Island Sound on the night of February 11, 1907. Though the night sky was clear, a strong gale blew out of the northwest. Emerging from the dark, the schooner H.P. Knowlton sailed directly toward the Larchmont. Attempting to avoid the onrushing ship, the steamer's pilot, John Anson, inadvertently turned the 1605-ton paddlewheeler into the path of the schooner. Seconds later, the two collided sending the Larchmont to the bottom within 12 minutes. Two hundred lives were lost that night and only seventeen survived. Those that made it to Block Island went ashore with their dead companions encased in ice. The Harry P. Knowlton struggled toward shore and went aground at Quonochontaug Beach, on the south shore of Rhode Island.

The Larchmont lies approximately 3.5 miles southeast of Watch Hill. Resting on a gravel bottom at about 130 feet, the nearly intact

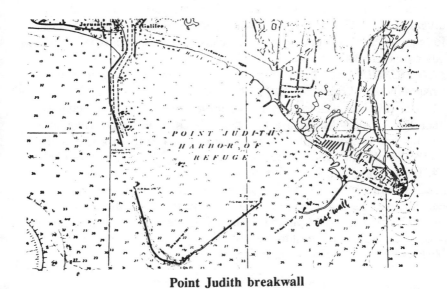

Point Judith breakwall

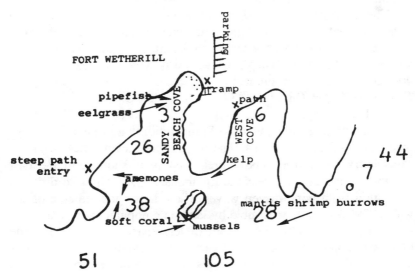

Fort Wetherill

83

ship is not for the inexperienced diver. Currents are strong, with low visibility a general rule. It is best to dive the wreck with a tether line attached to the anchor line. This will facilitate returning to the anchor line in a situation that is usually a decompression dive. Salvage divers will be delighted with the wreck, since there is still much to be found. Underwater photographers would be more satisfied with other area wrecks.

TUG HERCULES
Source: Frank Johnson
Chart #13205   Loran: 14593.0 25973.7 43953.6

The Hercules was located and identified by then SCUBA charter operator, Frank Johnson. He had been asked to unsnag a draggers net that had become fouled on the wreck. The 150-ton tug was built in 1880 and sank when it struck a submerged object on December 14, 1903. Upright in 95 feet of water, the vessel is located about two nautical miles south of Weekapaug Point. Other than the loss of its wheelhouse, the tug is largely intact. Plenty is left on the wreck for souvenir hunters. An average visibility of less than 15 feet and strong current, make it best to always dive the tug with a tether line.

HEROINE (S-W of Point Judith, R. I.)
Chart #13205
Loran: 14525.7(8) 43935.9

The freighter Heroine sank of unknown causes, 3.5 nautical miles south of Green Hill Point. The deterioating steel vessel lies in approximately 80 feet of water. Currents are sometimes strong at the wreck, on a falling or rising tide. Visibility which ranges from 10 to 40+ feet, is best in late summer.

POINT JUDITH BREAKWATER (Pt. Judith, R.I.)
Chart #13219, 13218

There are three breakwalls at Point Judith that protect the harbor from the ravages of the sea. The west breakwall reaches out from Jerusalem's shore, the central breakwall is offshore, and the east breakwall touches land near the lighthouse. The walls afford divers protection from wind-driven waves when diving the lee side of the walls. The east wall, accessible by land, is a popular spot on a warm summer's day. The shallow depth of less than 15 feet, makes the breakwall appropriate for new divers and snorklers alike. The rocks are covered with seaweed, barnacles, small anemones and tunicates (sea squirts). Lobster and occasional blue crab inhabit the rocks with tautog (blackfish) and cunner. The seaward side of all three walls are host to larger, migratory species, such as bluefish and striped bass.

The west and central breakwalls are more easily dived by boat. It is also probably best to dive only the west side of the west wall, since boating traffic and current present a major problem on the opposite side. At each of the walls, lines from the *many* lobster traps can easily entangle a diver. Watch also for fishing lines. Visibility at the breakwalls depends mostly upon wind direction and time of year. It varies between 5 to 25+ feet.

UNNAMED WRECK
Chart #13218
Loran: 43940.4 14455.3

Sitting in 99 feet of water and rising 33 feet off the bottom, the surfaces of the unnamed wreck are covered with marine growth. It is situated southeast of Point Judith.

SS BLACK POINT (stern)
Chart #13218
Loran: 14456.2 43938.5

The 5,353-ton coal hauler SS Black Point, sailing from a southeasterly direction through Block Island Sound, was the last victim of the German sub, U-853. Four days prior to the European Armistice, on May 5, 1945, a torpedo tore through the Black Point, breaking it in two and sending it to the bottom. Sinking in less than 15 minutes, 34 of its crew made their escape but 12 perished. The vessel lies about 3 miles southeast of Point Judith Light, in 80 to 90 feet of water.

Captain Bill Palmer of the Pilotfish, a SCUBA charter out of Snug Harbor, R.I., was the first to locate the wreck. He did so with the aid of his side scan sonar and a lot of research. When first dived, munitions from the ship's gun were scattered all around the deck. The popular wreck is considerably "picked over," through relics are still found.

The Black Point's stern gun is an awesome sight as you descend the anchor line. Though thoroughly covered with marine life, the armament is easily recognizable. The freighter's bulkheads are gradually falling away, making entry easy.

The entire stern is covered with frilled anemones, pink hydroids and bryozoans. Sea raven, large cunner, American eel, eelpout, hake, lobster and occasional cod, make their home on the wreckage.

Visibility can vary from 10 to 60 feet with the best clarity in late summer when the Gulf Stream turns in close to the shore. The chief hazards are debris and a diver himself. With a short bottom time, the interesting dive can easily become a decompression dive if time is not monitored carefully.

SUBMARINE, L-8
Chart #13218

Loran: 25776.0 43959.0 14424.4

Charted as cleared by wire drag at 85 feet, the L-8 was located by veteran wreck diver, Bill Palmer. Built in 1915 at the Portsmouth Naval Shipyard, the sub was capable of remaining submerged for the distance of only 150 miles, at a speed of 5 knots. Its submerged top speed was 10.5 knots. Armed with 4 torpedo tubes, it was meant for coastal duty only. In 1926, the Navy used the sub for target practice, sending it to the bottom with the first US use of a magnetic torpedo.

Lying on its port side in about 105 feet of water south of the Brenton Reef Light, the sub is a "dark" wreck, with only limited visibility. Little of value is left on the sub. Marine life abounds, though underwater photographers would have better luck on the nearby Black Point.

L-8

STATE PIER # 5 - Narragansett
Chart #13223, 13219

The pier at Narragansett is an easy entry dive into relatively shallow water. After parking right at the pier, enter via the beach. Away from the pier, the bottom drops off to 25+ feet. The sea floor is sand and rock with plenty of hiding places for that great tasting crustacean, the lobster. Tautog, cunner, striped bass, flatfish and occasional skate are seen. Blood starfish is often on the underside of the rocks.

Hazards include boat traffic and current. Onshore waves can ruin the visibility that varies from 5 to 25+ feet.

RHODE ISLAND
Chart #13223 (see area chart)

On November 6, 1880, the steamer Rhode Island struck the

86

rocks at Bonnet Point, in a heavy fog. Held fast on the reef, the sea ultimately broke the 325-foot sidewheeler's back and it began breaking up. Though it is still indicated on the navigational charts, little or no structure is left. It takes a great deal of time and patience to find anything, though it is no doubt worth the effort. Current can be very strong at the site and, due to silt, visibility is ordinarily not very good.

BEAVERTAIL POINT STATE PARK - Captain Lawrence
Chart #313223 (Jamestown, R.I. - Conanicut Island)

First built in 1749 and rebuilt in 1856, the lighthouse at Beavertail is the focal point of the park. The site is an ideal place for a host of family activities.

Rocks of all sizes encircle the point, forming canyons alive with marine life. To the west, the bottom drops off to about 45 feet. At the point itself, a small natural channel cuts through the rocks in a SW direction, leading to the fishing boat, Captain Lawrence. The wreck which is in 30 feet of water, 175 feet from shore, consists of beams and plating. It is host to cunner and tautog. Farther out on the point and on the east side, divers often spear striped bass. Cod, squirrel hake (ling), and skate are just some of the more unusual fish seen here. The sea floor on the east side of the point slopes down much faster than the opposite side. The entire area, however, can provide great diving.

The greatest hazard at Beavertail is the surge produced by onshore waves, with a potential of being deadly! *The only time to dive the location* is in calm seas. Good alternates are Fort Wetherill (#1) or Fort Getty (#2).

FORT GETTY
Chart #13223 (Jamestown, R. I.)

Fort Getty is a spot that is used by out-of-state divers more for camping, than for diving. From the campground, all of Rhode Island's beach access dive sites are in easy reach. In addition, there are rest rooms, showers and a boat ramp. You cannot reserve a camp site; its first come, first served.

The diving here, is probably best called, last resort.In shallow, near shore water, oyster toadfish, rock eel and small crabs hide under the rocks. Farther offshore, the sandy bottom is home for numerous flatfish and hermit crabs. The bottom overall however, is

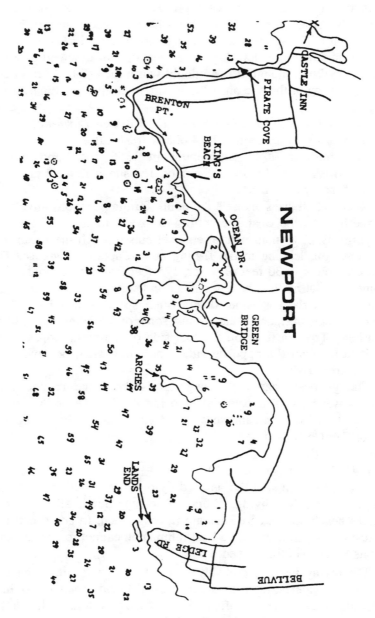

Newport, Rhode Island

uninteresting. Current is *strong* at the north point, with boat traffic a constant problem, especially on weekends.

FORT WETHERILL
Chart #13223 (Jamestown, R.I.)

Located at the southeast end of Conanicut Island, Fort Wetherill is a great place to explore and picnic, with adequate room for most outdoor activities. It is a perfect family dive site, with plenty to keep the kids and the non-divers busy. Fresh water and rest rooms are available at the fort.

Sandy Beach Cover (see chart) is accessible from the parking lot which forms a u-turn, high above the cove. Entry here involves a steep and difficult bank that, however, quickly leads to open water. An easier entry to the cove is via the concrete boat ramp next to the service building. That area of Sandy Beach Cove is shallow and mostly eelgrass, requiring a long snorkel before reaching the more interesting bottom. Small lobster and pipefish, including occasional tropicals, inhabit the eelgrass area.

On the opposite (east) side of the service building, a narrow path leads to West Cove. (A boat launch ramp has been proposed for that area). Kelp and Irish moss line most of West Cove's shoreline with frilled anemones, mud anemones, star coral and soft coral in deeper water, The same animals dwell in Sandy Cove, especially on its west wall. Lobster, blackfish and cunner are always present. If a diver is especially observant, a mantis shrimp with its emerald colored, stalked eyes, can be seen at its burrow.

The main hazard at the fort is the long snorkel. A wise diver will begin to return underwater while there is enough air left to do so. Current is not a problem within the coves. Visibility ranging from 5 to 30 feet, depends a lot on wind direction and plankton blooms.

HOPE ISLAND WRECK
Chart #13223 (Narragansett Bay)

On the south side of Hope Island, Indicated on the charts as "boiler awash," (buoy RG), lies the reminants of what some believe to be the Beaver Tail ferry or a tug.

Built in 1896, the 110-foot long Beaver Tail ran between Jamestown and Saunderstown. By 1923, the ferry was deemed inadequate to carry auto traffic, thus, from that time, it was used as a "spare" on the same run. With a major hurricane headed for the area on September 21, 1938, the vessel was sailed for the protection of Newport Harbor. Having difficulties with its boiler, it anchored near Gould Island. The anchor did not hold, and the ship was washed ashore on the northeast end of Jamestown. On December 30, 1938, the vessel was sold as scrap for $210.00.

The unidentified Hope Island wreck, which may be a tug, lies in very shallow water. Visibility in the area, never good, is usually best on a flood tide.

CASTLE HILL Newport, R.I.

Chart #13223

Alexander Agassiz, a world famous oceanographer and marine biologist, built his summer home at Castle Hill, in 1874. It is now the Inn at Castle Hill. The scientist is often quoted as having said that the local shores were ideal for the study of marine animals. In 1890, a lighthouse was built at Castle Hill on land deeded by Agassiz, to the US, for the sum of $1.00. Just off the light, is one of the better dive sites in the Newport area.

The only way to dive Castle Hill, if you are not a guest of the Inn, is by boat. (Some manage to carry their equipment up the access road, from the parking lot next to the Coast Guard station) A shallow cove, less than 100 yards north of the light, is a good place to secure a Zodiac type of watercraft. Otherwise, stay slightly offshore, checking the depth with a sounder. Close to shore, the boulder strewn bottom could easily make your boat the latest wreck dive. (Don't forget to get a Loran fix for the rest of us, before it sinks!) *Current* is a significant hazard at this site. Maximum flow is 2.5 hours before ebb (high tide) or 3 hours after. The velocity of the current varies between 1.5 to 2 knots, thus dive only at slack.

The bottom at Castle Hill slopes from 10 to 180 feet, in less than 100 yards. The boulders which line the shoreline become more sparse as you descend, with wide expanses of gravel bottom. Stony corals, tiny lined anemones, *Fagesia lineata,* and frilled anemones cover nearly every rock. Large tautog and their near relatives, cunner, are always present. Cod, ling and goosefish are sometimes also seen. Best of all, legal-sized lobster are common, below 40 feet.

LYDIA SKOLFIELD (Newport, R.I.)

Chart #13223

On the morning of Sunday, April 19, 1891, the Lydia Skolfield, loaded with 7,000 barrels of cotton seed oil, ran aground on Butterball Rock. Most of the three-masted schooner's cargo was saved before it broke up three months later. Some of its decking was washed ashore with other sections remaining at the site.

According to Jim Jenny, "In Search of Shipwrecks," the remains lie about 100 yards offshore, on the east side of Butterball Rock.

PIRATE COVE (Ocean Drive, Newport, R.I.)
Chart #13223

Parking at this dive site is limited to the nearby lot at Breton Point State Park. Drop off your equipment and walk back the 2/10 of a mile. Entry is at the south side of the point, down a gully.

Near shore, rock crevices and boulders line the bottom. Farther out, there are wide areas of sand with patches of rock. Cunner, tautog and flatfish are always present. Current gets stronger as you move away from the shoreline. The site is poor with onshore waves.

KING'S BEACH (Ocean Drive, Newport, R.I.)
Chart #13223

If there ever was a place for check-out dives and open water dives, Kings Beach is it. As the most popular spot in Newport, at

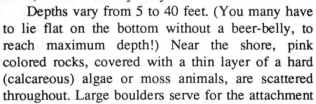

times, it can only be described as wall-to-wall divers. A concrete launch ramp, suited only to small boats, makes it an easy entry.

Depths vary from 5 to 40 feet. (You many have to lie flat on the bottom without a beer-belly, to reach maximum depth!) Near the shore, pink colored rocks, covered with a thin layer of a hard (calcareous) algae or moss animals, are scattered throughout. Large boulders serve for the attachment of various sea weeds, including kelp. Under some of the medium sized boulders, small lobsters, crabs, sea squirts, blood stars and tube worms make their home. Tautog, cunner and flatfish are common.

GREEN BRIDGE (Ocean Drive, Newport, R.I.)
Chart #13223

The very shallow dive site is a favorite with tropical fish collectors. Late August is the best time to find the out-of-place creatures.

ARCHES: GOOSEBERRY ISLAND
Chart #13223   Source: Darlene Tomalis
Loran: 25761.8 43911.6

This dive is not for beginners. The surge can be very dangerous in the vicinity of these beautiful, naturally formed arches.

Anchor on the southwest side of Gooseberry Island, in about 40 feet of water. Leave plenty of scope on the anchor, securing it well, since ocean rollers could otherwise pick it up. Swimming for the largest rock on the southwest end of the island, dive to about 2/3 of the way to the bottom. In that vicinity, you should find the first arch; the second is just beyond. *Dive the Arches only in calm seas.*

LLEWELLYN HOWLAND
Chart #13223 (Seal Ledge, Newport, R.I.)

The tanker Llewellyn Holland of the Bayland Line, was bound for Portland, Maine on the beautiful clear morning of April 21, 1924. Loaded with 26,000 barrels of oil, the ship's master, Captain Larson, cut too close to the shore and went aground on Seal Ledge. Built of iron by the Morgan Iron Works in 1888, the 36-year-old ship immediately began leaking oil, bathing the nearby shoreline. Attempts were made to transfer its cargo to barges, but they were of no avail. It was finally decided to burn the oil, and on May 3, 1924, a fire was started that continued to burn for several days. Reduced to a charred hulk, the 283-foot tanker gradually broke up and settled to the bottom at Seal Ledge.

The wreck is reported by Jim Jenny "In Search of Shipwrecks" as "resting in 26 to 32 feet of water at the west side of Seal Ledge, about 500 feet SW from the shallowest spot of 17 feet and 500 feet NW of the south tip where it is 23 feet." The twisted metal structures have become a habitat for many marine creatures.

LAND'S END (Off Bellvue Avenue, Newport, R.I.)
Chart #13223, 13218

Bellvue Avenue in Newport, is best known for its famous mansions. The extreme south end of Bellvue is crossed by Ledge Road, that leads to a quiet dive site, Land's End. After turning down Ledge toward the water, park on the right side of the road. Land's End is a well protected lagoon with a maximum depth of less than 15 feet. The bottom is covered by rocks of various sizes among which tropical fish hide in late summer. To go deeper, you must swim to

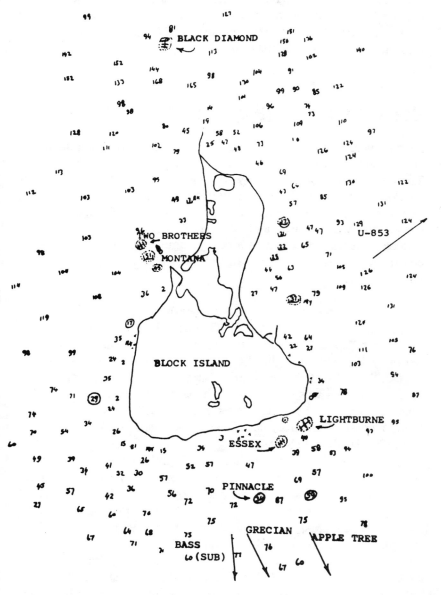

Block Island wrecks

93

the exposed south side of the offshore rocks that form the lagoon. The ocean swells on the outside can be a challenge for even the most experienced diver, but on a calm day, diving here is superb! The deep crevices and ledges that harbor large tautog and striped bass, make it a favorite of spearfishermen.

BLOCK ISLAND (Rhode Island)

Block Island which lies about 10 miles southwest of Point Judith, is surrounded by some of the most interesting Northeast shipwrecks. Though Loran is not necessary to locate the popular Lightburne, it would be almost impossible to find others without a unit. As with any offshore site, be sure to equip the boat with a VHF marine radio, (forget the CB!), flares and extra fuel, being sure to check the weather forecast. If caught in a heavy summer fog that is typical of coastal Rhode Island, the Loran unit will also help get you safely back to shore.

TANKER LIGHTBURNE (Block Island)
Chart #13205   Loran: 14535.6(7) 43872.6(4.7-8)
The 6,429-ton Texaco tanker Lightburne ran aground on February 10, 1939, in sight of the lighthouse, at the southeast end of Block Island. Loaded with 72,000 barrels of kerosene and gasoline, some of the fuel was saved before the ship was given up to the sea. Fourteen years earlier, the tanker had rescued three men off the Florida coast. The three, near death, had been adrift for nearly a month in a small open boat.

The Coast Guard dynamited the Lightburne in an effort to eliminate it as a navigational hazard. Luckily, they were not totally successful. The ship's remains are scattered over a large area in 30 feet of water. The ship's ribs have taken on the appearance of well-groomed courtyards, on whose fences grow a variety of life. The structures are covered with colonies of northern star coral and different species of sea weed, barnacle, anemone and starfish. In the larger, center section, a ladder leads to the deck above. A diver's light will reveal frilled anemones clinging to the ceiling and bulkheads. Schools of juvenile cunner seek protection on the wreck. Tautog (blackfish), American and conger eel, including a variety of open water fish, make opportune targets for spearfishing divers.

The wreck is well marked on the navigational charts. It is about 400 feet shoreward of buoy C-1, and slightly east of the lighthouse. The Lightburne's outline can be seen from the surface on a calm, sunny day, the best time to dive the site. Waves at this shallow depth pick up the sandy bottom, limiting visibility, which ranges from 10 to 25+ feet.

STEAMER ESSEX (Block Island)
Chart #13205   Loran: 43872.3(4) 25838.0(7.7) 14536.8

Sailing from Lisbon to New York, the steamer Essex ran aground on September 25, 1941, at the southeast end of Block Island. It did so in almost the very same spot as did the ill-fated Lightburne,some two years earlier. The area's treacherous shoreline also nearly claimed the Malamton out of Jacksonville, Florida, in April of 1938. The freighter was refloated and towed to New York for repair. The Essex was not so fortunate. It stayed aground with its cargo until all was lost in a December storm. Wind and waves crushed its superstructure, as cargo and ship were scattered on the sandy bottom. Lying in 25 to 30 feet of water, a short distance west of the Lightburne, little of anything recognizable remains of the vessel. The wreckage of the 90-ton freighter does still provide some brass souvenirs which becomes uncovered in the shifting sands. Parts of the Essex are colonized with marine life, though the Lightburne is more luxuriant.

Visibility at the wreck varies between 10 to 20+ feet, depending on the seas. The site is easily reached by private boat, though it would be difficult to locate without Loran.

PINNACLE (Block Island)
Chart #13205   Loran: 45865.0(6.7-8) 25884.9(8) 14547.6

Pushed ahead of an advancing glacier, the terminal moraine, made up of huge boulders, spreads over almost 1/2 acre. Lying approximately 2.5 miles off the southwest point of Block Island, the site is one of the most interesting dives in the Northeast. The rocks rise 35 or more feet off the bottom, resembling underwater cliffs. They form tunnels, caves and crevices that can be easily negotiated by a diver. All forms of marine life compete for space on the exposed surfaces, with large schools of fish making their residence among the rocks. The Pinnacle should delight sightseers, marine biologists and underwater photographers.

Depths at the Pinnacle range from 35 to 75 feet. Visibility can be as good as 40 to 60 feet, though it can be as little as 10 feet. Be sure to watch for current, and have someone stay aboard the boat while others are below.

SCHOONER MONTANA   Source: Frank Johnson
Chart #13205   Loran: 43900.7(3) 25871.2(1.8) 14546.0

Laden with a cargo of lumber and coal, the schooner Montana floundered a quarter mile west of Block Island, on January 21, 1907. Locally known as the "coal pile," the ship lies on a sandy bottom that slopes from 75 to 90 feet. Other than souvenirs of coal, salvage divers will find slim pickings on the wreck. Underwater photographers and sightseers will, however, be more than satisfied with the prolific marine life making its home among the rib structures of the 165 foot schooner. Eel pout, conger and American eel, cunner and tautog, all inhabit the wreck. Anemones are particularly plentiful on the ship's beams.

Current is not usually a problem, with visibility averaging 10 to 20+ feet. The structure is difficult to locate without Loran and a chart recorder; without these, a SCUBA charter is the easiest way to dive the Montana.

TWO BROTHERS   (Block Island)
Chart #13205   Loran: 43902.3(2) 25872.1(3) 14546.0

The wooden schooner was located by Frank Johnson, in 1976, with his charter boat, Hey Bo. Buried almost to its deck in sand and lying in 95 feet of water, the wreck was tentatively identified by him as the schooner, "Two Brothers."

BLACK DIAMOND   (Block Island)
Chart #13205   Loran: 43930.6(8) 25875.5(4)

The wreck lies within a short distance north of Block Island North Reef, in approximately 80 feet.

U-853   (Block Island)
Chart #13218   Loran: 14472.9 43895.1(4.9) 25998.1

Commissioned on June 25, 1943, the 252 foot-long German submarine joined the Battle of the Atlantic after several months of sea trials. Under the command of Helmet Sommer, the 750-ton sub nearly sank on June 18, 1944, when it came under fire of a Hunter-Killer Group. Commander Sommer was wounded on the bridge but despite his wounds, he dove the vessel and eluded his attackers, returning to Germany for refitting.

In February of 1945, the U-853 arrived at its new operating area, off the southern New England coast. On May 5, 1945, the submarine fired its last torpedo, sending the SS Black Point to the bottom, and sealing its own fate as well. Sailing in the vicinity, the freighter, the SS Kamen, sounded the alarm. It was picked up by the Coast Guard frigate, Moberly, that was travelling nearby in company of two Navy destroyers, the Amik and the Atherton. Directed by the Moberly, the ships began a search pattern. At 2014 (8:14 pm), two hours after the sinking of the Black Point, the Atherton made sonar

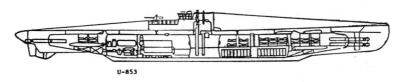

U-853

contact with the U-853. Within a short time, the destroyer had dropped 13 magnetic mines, one of which exploded. Two more attacks were carried out before the "brass" were convinced of their "kill." Following the war, the crew's remains were removed and returned to Germany.

The sub sits upright on a sand bottom, in about 120 to 125 feet of water. The deck is at 110 feet. Descending on the anchor line, visibility is dramatically reduced as you enter a thermocline. Farther down, there is an eerie sensation as the shape of the U-853 emerges from the dark. Water clarity at the bottom ranges from 5 to 40+ feet.

Much of the vessel's outer hull has deteriorated leaving pipes and metal framework exposed. For souvenir hunters, the often visited sub can still yield worthwhile finds. Of the resident marine fish, the sea raven is second in number only to the cunner. The hundreds of frilled anemones that cover almost every available surface, leave a mucous film on your wet suit. Above all however, a visit to the U-853 can certainly be called a "dive into history."

SS GRECIAN   (Block Island)
Chart #13205   Loran: 43830.8 25823.8 14542.7(6.7) (?)

Sailing with a general cargo from Boston to Norfolk on May 27, 1932, the SS Grecian collided with the City of Chattanooga, in a thick fog. Striking the Grecian just aft of the smoke stack, the captain of the Chattanooga was able to keep the bow of his ship in the Grecian's side long enough for 30 of the ill-fated ship's crew, to make their escape. Thirty minutes after the accident, the Grecian slid to the sea floor, taking with it, the four remaining crewmen.

The steel freighter is scattered on the bottom, resembling more a junkyard than what was once a 263-foot ship, with a 29-foot beam. It is however, great pickings for salvage divers and marine life buffs. Brass is often found, and sea creatures grow on every exposed surface of the ship. Goosefish are often seen away from the wreck.

APPLE TREE WRECK   (Block Island)
Chart #13205   Loran: 43836.5 14540.0

The unidentified wreck lies in 85 feet of water, less than a mile from the Grecian.

USS BASS   (Block Island)
Chart #13205   Loran: 14560.8 43817.4

Built in 1924 at the Portsmouth Naval Shipyard, the USS Bass was one of three similar V Class submarines called collectively "B"

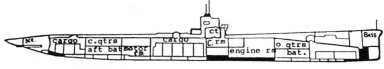

USS BASS

boats. The Navy brass had high hopes for the 341-foot submarines, but because of various technical difficulties, all were decommissioned before the end of World War II. During the last of four wartime patrols in the Pacific, fire broke out aboard the Bass, asphyxiating 26 enlisted men. The sub was then converted to a sub-cargo carrier, not meeting with success in that role either. On March 12, 1945, the sub was stripped of its gear and deliberately sunk off Block Island. The Navy then used the ship as a sonar target.

The Bass lies in 150 feet of water, 7.5 miles from Block Island's Southeast Point Light, on a course of 178.5° true. The bow sits directly south of the conning tower, in a bed of sand. The structure is

98

Grécian: Courtesy Mariners Museum, Newport News, Va.

USS BASS: National Archives Collection, #80-G-423378

Oregon: Courtesy Mariners Museum, Newport News, Va.

San Diego: National Archives Collection #19-N-13904
(Formerly U.S.S. California)

USS Turner: National Archives Collection #80-G-84344

Gulftrade: Courtesy Peabody Museum of Salem

101

Typical souvenirs off the San Diego:
Andy Pawlowski collection

upright, with props and antennae still intact. The entire sub is remarkably free of marine growth, though numerous cunner and hake frequent the site . Large lobster and an occasional deep sea scallop are found on the wreck. Because of the depth, the Bass should be dived by the experienced only.

OFFSHORE WRECKS

Offshore wrecks are out-of-reach to most private boats except for the larger 30 to 50-foot vessels. Even those can feel like a dinghy when confronted with a sudden Atlantic storm. Thus, for most, offshore shipwrecks should be dived from a well operated charter boat. Because all of the wrecks are deep and at considerable distances from shore, it would be wise to have oxygen available for the emergency treatment of the bends, along with the usual ship-board emergency equipment.

ANDREA DORIA
Source: AWOIS

Chart #13003Loran: 14080.9 43481.7
Lat/Long 40/29/30 69/50/36

Steaming toward New York on July 25, 1956, the Andrea Doria entered a fog bank, 50 miles south of Nantucket Island. Having left New York earlier that day, the Swedish motor vessel, Stockholm, proceeding east, was itself engulfed in the same fog. Despite modern radar, the two collided, the motor vessel's ice breaking bow cutting an 80-foot hole into the forward section of the Doria. Empty fuel tanks and the generator room quickly filled with sea water, rolling the Queen of the Italian line over to its starboard side. The luxury liner stayed afloat for 11 hours before finally surrendering to the sea. Most of the 1,709 passengers were rescued, yet the Doria continues to take lives. Divers, poorly prepared for an excursion to well beyond sport diving depth, have been lost on the 170 to 225+ foot deep wreck. Though many more divers have been lost in much shallower water, only the well trained,equipped and experienced should attempt the Andrea Doria.

Description of passenger decks, starting from the uppermost deck (see line drawing, page 104)

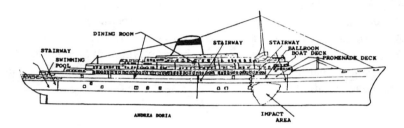

Andrea Doria: The Doria's stack was painted red, white and green, the national colors of Italy.

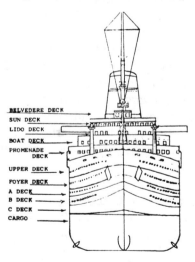

Andrea Doria: Drawings modified from illustrations by Edward H. Wiswesser, Warship Drawings

Belvedere Deck: top deck located just below the stack.

Sun Deck: wheelhouse

Lido Deck; gym, massage parlor, solarium, swimming pool, bar,playroom and officers quarters.

Boat Deck: lifeboats, open promenade and lounge.

Promenade Deck: enclosed by large windows, lounges, ballrooms and passenger cabins.

Upper deck: first class cabins

Foyer deck: purser's office, bank, shops and chapel

A Deck: cabins and ship's hospital

B Deck: engine room, and auto garage

C Deck: engine room

Cargo holds here

COIMBRA   Source: AWOIS

Chart #13003   Loran: 43576.6(3-4) 26203.6(9-4.0)

Lat/Long: 40/23/12 72/21/30

During the first half of 1942, the East Coast became an intensive and successful hunting ground for U-boats. The first victims claimed that year off the Atlantic coast of New York and New Jersey, were the 9.577-ton Panamanian tanker Norness, sunk on January 14, 1942 and the 6,768-ton British tanker Coimbra, sunk on the next day.

The Coimbra was en route for New York Harbor when it was attacked by a German submarine, 28 miles off Southampton, N. Y. Ironically, the ship had been built in 1937 by the Howaldswerke Company of Kiel, Germany. The 423-foot tanker went immediately to the bottom, breaking up into three sections. Some of the crew made it to safety but most perished with the ship. The wreckage lies in 185+ feet of water.

VARANGER   Source(s):John Raguso*

Chart #12318   Rick Lippert

Loran: 42804.1(3.8) 26825.2(3.5)

The Norwegian tanker Varanger was built in 1925, at Amsterdam. In January of 1942, the vessel became the sixth victim of U-boat attack on the Atlantic coast during that month. Having picked up a full load of fuel oil in Africa and the West Indies, the Varanger was bound for New York. At about 3:00 am on January

25, 1942, the ship was struck by a torpedo. A few minutes later, the 9,305 gross ton vessel was hit by a second torpedo. That was followed five minutes later by still another, which sent the Varanger immediately to the bottom. The crewmen, all of whom survived, were picked up by two fishing boats, the San Gennaro and the Eileen.

The wreck lies 32 miles off Hereford Inlet, in 129 feet of water, rising to 74 feet. Though some of its bulkheads have deteriorated, the Varanger is relatively intact. Much of the structure is covered with marine life. Cod, cunner, lobster and eelpout make their home above and below the wreck.

*Raguso, J. 1985. Atlantic wreck series. Fisherman, 20: 14-17

TEXAS TOWER #4

Source(s): AWOIS
John Raguso*

Chart #13003
Loran: 26313.4 43266.6-9

Built in the late 1950's as part of the Early Warning Radar System, Texas Tower #4 was haunted by structural problems from the start. Standing in 186 feet of water, its lower deck housed the power plant. The tower's middle deck served as the crew's quarters and the upper deck held radar equipment. Even when the facility was in relatively good shape, it sometimes swayed as much as 14 feet, giving it the name of "Old Shaky." In 1958 and again in 1960, the tower was battered by hurricanes, setting the scene for its demise. On January 15, 1961, a winter storm that had begun three days earlier, rocked the structure to the point of collapse, trapping the crew of 25.

The radar platform is readily accessible to divers beginning at a depth of about 70 feet. Entry is easy through the structure's doorways, though it should be done with a penetration line. On a clear day, a diver can see down some of the tower's passageways even without a dive light! On that type of day, you may also be able to see the bottom of the wreck, from its highest point. Visibility on the wreck is generally best at mid-day, in calm seas, when the site is being "washed" by the Gulf Stream.

Frilled anemones and hydroids are attached to the tower's bulkheads with schools of cunner swimming in and out of the wreck. Cod, ling, bluefish and many other varieties of fish frequent the sunken tower, with an occasional shark or ocean sunfish, *Mola*

mola. Souvenir hunters should not be disappointed as there is plenty to take home and display. The greatest drawback to the site is its distance from shore, 57 miles off Fire Island.

*Raguso, J. 1985. Atlantic wreck series. Fisherman 20: 14-17

STOLT DAGALI   Sources:John Raguso*
Chart #13003   Loran: 26768.0 43410.0

Running in a heavy fog, just after 2:00 am on November 26, 1964, the Norwegian tanker Stolt Dagali collided with the Israeli liner, Shalom. In the impact, the Shalom cut the Dagali in two, sending the tanker's stern immediately to the bottom. The bow remained afloat and was towed to port for salvage. The crippled Shalom, with a 40-foot gash in its bow, made its own way back to port.

The popular wreck lies in 130 feet of water, rising 60 feet off the bottom. Frilled anemones have colonized much of its exposed surfaces with small patches of northern star coral and soft coral occupying any available niche. Lobstering is generally good, with cod, ling, eelpout, and large schools of baitfish seeking safety on the wreck. Visibility ranges from about 20 to 60+ feet.

*Raguso, J. 1985. Atlantic wreck series. Fisherman 20: 14-17

R.P. RESOR   Source: Rick Lippert
Chart #13003   Loran: 26638.4(3) 43277.2(1-3)

On February 26, 1942, a German U-boat waited patiently in the dark early morning hours, off the coast of New Jersey. As its quarry came into range, the sub fired its torpedoes, one of which found its mark on the port side of the ship. The 7,451-ton tanker R.P. Resor, bound for Fall River, Massachusetts, was immediately set ablaze. The stricken vessel, loaded with 79,000 barrels of oil, burned and drifted for over a day before finally going to the bottom off Barnegat Inlet. Only two crewmen survived; the ship's captain Fred Marcus and 47 other crewmen were lost.

The badly broken up wreck lies in 125 feet of water, with only the stern and a portion of the bow still intact. The ship's structure has become a haven for cod, eelpout, cunner and lobster. Many of the exposed surfaces are covered with anemones, hydroids and small colonies of northern star coral. Sharks are sometimes seen at the site.

Visibility which varies between 10 to 60+ feet, is often best in late summer.

LONG ISLAND - SOUTH SHORE

The majority of shipwrecks off the south shore of Long Island occurred early in the island's history. The wrecks, whose locations are known, have long been used as favorite fishing spots, the decaying structures providing an attractive habitat for blackfish (tautog) and other species. Unfortunately, many of the older shipwrecks have been lost to shifting sands and other natural processes of the sea. Of the south shore wrecks, the most often dived are probably the Black Warrior, 1859, the Oregon, 1886, and the San Diego, 1918.

SNUG HARBOR   (off Montauk Point, N.Y.)   Source: AWOIS
Chart #13205   Loran: 14647.07 25942.54 43842.99 60095.77
On August 20, 1920, the Snug Harbor was making its way in a heavy fog, four miles southeast of Montauk Point. Without the availability of radar, the 2,388-ton steel vessel did not see the barge Pottsville, being towed by the tug Covington, until it was too late. Unable to avoid the barge, the two collided and the snug Harbor immediately began taking on water. The tug was able to rescue all of the Snug Harbor's crew, including the daughter of one of the ship's officer's, before the ill-fated vessel went to the bottom.

The wreck lies in about 60 feet of water, east of Montauk Shoal; the whereabouts of the Pottsville is unknown.

JENNINGS POINT - USS OHIO   Source: Ron Zaleski
Chart #12358   7Z'z Hampton Bay Divers
Jennings Point on Shelter Island, New York, can be reached by boat or car. Access to the island is via ferry, leaving from Greenport every 1/2 hour.

The entire point is bounded by rocks. The depth drops off very rapidly from shore to 50 to 60 feet. At that depth, approximately 300 yards offshore, lies and unidentified wreck. Old bottles and some anchors are the normal find at the site. Some fish are seen, though other areas are better. Hazards include boat traffic and strong surface currents.

Just across the water from Jennings Point, at Conkling Point, lies remnants of the 212-foot long USS Ohio. Sold for scrap after over a half-century of service, the 1820-warship was brought to Greenport in 1884, and salvaged. Some of its structure sits in less than 20 feet of water, off the point.

NOYACK BAY WRECK (N.Y.)   Source: Ron Zaleski
Chart #12358   (North Haven Peninsula)   7Z's

A World War I barge, which caught fire and sank, lies 150 feet offshore in the far east corner of Noyack Bay. The wreck sits upright in 15 feet of water, straight off a cement pad, as indicated on the charts. The barge was used in torpedo run trials, aiming the torpedoes toward a 1000-foot net. Some of the old dummy warheads are buried in the bottom of the bay. Ron Zaleski, dive shop owner, recovered one and has it on display at his shop.

MONTAUK JETTIES
Chart #13209

Both jetties leading out of Lake Montauk are good dive sites. The large rocks which form the jetties are habitat for blackfish, cunner and lobster. The lake itself supports blue eyed (bay) scallops which are not only good to eat, but great to photograph.

TENNYSON
Chart #13205   Loran: 26128.9 43793.8

The schooner Tennyson sank about 5.5 miles off East Hampton, New York, in 110 feet of water.

TUG PANTHER
Chart #13205   Loran: 26249.7 43802.0

The wreck which is said to be the tug Panther, lies 3 miles off Southampton, New York, in 90 feet of water.

OREGON
Chart #12353   Loran: 26452.7(9) 43676.3 stern
              26453.0(2) 43676.2 mid-ship
              26453.0(2) 43676.5(6) bow

Built in 1883 for the Guion Steamship Company, and then sold to Cunard, the steel hull liner had engines that developed more than 12,000 horse power. The ship, a record holder in its day, once made the Atlantic crossing in 6 days, 9 hours and 22 minutes. Two hundred forty tons of coal per day were consumed by the luxury liner's nine boilers. The 502-foot long, 52-foot wide four masted steamer, could accommodate 340 first class, 92 second class and 1,100 steerage passengers. Decorations aboard the Oregon were

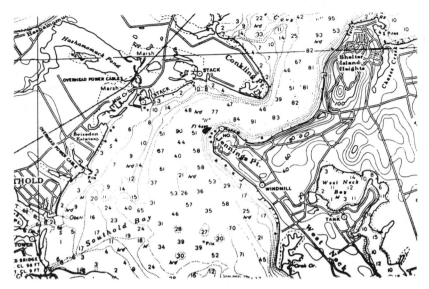

Jennings Point

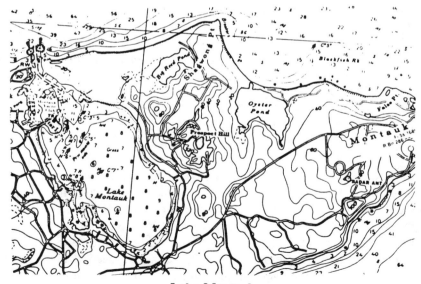

Lake Montauk

110

elaborate and the entire ship was illuminated with Edison incandescent lights.

At 4:20 am, on March 14, 1886, the Oregon was between Shinnecock and Fire Island, travelling at 18 knots toward New York. The ship's lookout spotted lights in the distance just before there was a loud, explosive noise which shook the liner from stem to stern. Water poured into the hole in the port side and within a short time, the pumps were overwhelmed. Distress rockets were fired and lifeboats launched which carried the 640 passengers and crew of 205 to safety. Eight hours later, the Oregon went to the bottom, bow first, in 130 feet of water. Speculation as to the cause of the accident included a possible blast from explosives in the cargo hold, ramming of the sunken Hylton Castle, or a collision with an unknown schooner. Examination of the manifest proved that there were no explosives aboard, and the Oregon was about 9 miles away from the Hylton Castle, at the time of the mishap. The day after the accident, the three masted schooner, Charles H. Morse, travelling from Baltimore to Boston, was reported overdue. Some time later, the 152-foot vessel was located southwest of Shinnecock Light, in 135 feet of water. All of the crew aboard the schooner had perished. Though the two wrecked vessels were 16.5 miles apart, the Oregon was known to have drifted considerably after the incident, as could have the Charles H. Morse.

Though much of the Oregon has broken up and collapsed to sea floor, parts, such as the boilers, are still intact. Divers continually retrieve a variety of souvenirs, from bricks to brass. Marine life is lush on the old structure, with a large number of fish including black bass, ling, cunner and an occasional goosefish. Lying in 130 feet of water, the Oregon is best dived by the more experienced.

WOLCOTT
Chart #12353   Loran: 26518.1(7) 43712.8(13.0)
           15146.8 59960.8

According to Jean Rattray, the unidentified wooden schooner was named by party boat Captain Freddy Wedge, when he discovered the wreck on the day that Wolcott beat Joe Louis. The wreck, which lies about 6 miles off Fire Island, is in 80+ feet of water.

SAN DIEGO   Source: Andy Pawlowski
Chart #12353   Loran: 26542.(2-9) 43692.9(3.3-8) 15173.3(9)

The 503-foot, 13,680-ton armored heavy cruiser San Diego, was capable of speeds of 22 knots (25mph). Built in 1903, the ship was first known as the California. As the pride of the Navy's armada, the warship was equipped with 4 eighteen-inch, 14 six-inch and 18 three-inch guns. It had a crew of 1200 officers and men.

On the morning of July 19, 1918, the San Diego was in route from Portsmouth Naval Shipyard to New York. As the cruiser passed southeast of Fire Island, there was a sudden explosion. A mine, laid by a German U-boat, did its work well. The first blast was soon followed by the rupture of the ship's boilers and then, its magazines. Within 25 minutes, the great warship rolled over and went to the bottom, taking a "belly-up" position on the sea floor.

The general structure of the decaying ship is still intact. Some plates have broken away, while others are loose, moving slightly up and down, and supported only by the metal grooves on which they lay. Entry is possible via gun ports, lost plates, rust holes or blast holes. A hole on the starboard side of the prop shaft, leads to a small arms storage area. Each room, however, can yield its own type of souvenir.

Photographers will be pleased with the large variety of sea life inhabiting the vessel. Anemones cling to every available surface, with both hard and soft coral occupying other spaces. Open water fish are often seen on the wreck.

The wreck rises to about 65 feet with a maximum depth of 110 feet. Visibility is often between 25 and 30 feet.

HYLTON (Hilton) CASTLE
Chart #12353   Loran: 26569.2(3) 43695.2

The sail and steam powered Hylton Castle was built in 1871 by Oswald and Company, at Sunderland, England. Loaded with a cargo of corn, the vessel set sail from New York on Friday, January 8, 1886, bound for France. On the following morning, the freight steamer found itself in the midst of a fierce winter storm. Waves broke over the ship from bow to stern, eventually tearing up the ship's rudder, all of its rigging, and all but two of its lifeboats. By Monday, the continually battered vessel, which was now almost entirely encased in ice, sprang a leak. Within a short time, Captain

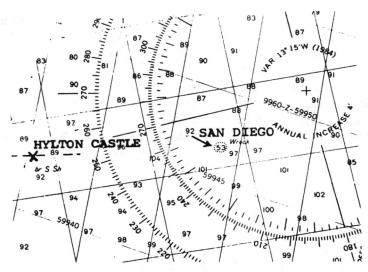

Wrecks: San Diego,. Hylton Castle

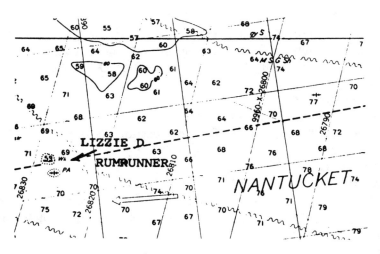

Wreck: Rumrunner—Lizzie D

113

Colvin had to order his crew to abandon the sinking ship. Two lifeboats were launched; nine men went with Mate John Marshall, the others boarded a boat with Captain Colvin. Mr. Marshall's lifeboat made its way to Fire Island Light with the crew's clothes covered with ice. The captain's boat, the heavier of the two, ran into much more difficulty. Soon after abandoning ship, the two lifeboats became separated. Early on, all except for one pair of oars broke on the captain's boat, preventing it from making much headway. Waves poured over the sides and often froze before the water could be bailed. As the sun set, the unfortunate sailors were still far offshore. Around 9:00 pm, a light was spotted in the distance that proved to be a fishing smack at anchor, the Stephen Woolsey. The men aboard the lifeboat cried out for help and a fisherman threw out a line. The half frozen men had been saved.

Lying in about 95 feet of water, 8 miles off Fire Island, the mass of wreckage does not, in any way, resemble a ship. The rusting structure does however, provide plenty of lobster and occasional souvenirs.

AIRPLANE
Chart #12353   Loran: 26605.9 43716.8

The unidentified aircraft, lies in approximately 75 feet of water, 6 miles off Ocean Beach.

DODGER
Chart #12353   Loran: 26618.0 43673.4

The unidentified wooden wreck was named "Dodger" by a party boat captain, when he located it on the day the Dodgers won the pennant. It is situated 10 miles southwest of Ocean Beach, New York, in 95 feet of water.

LIGHTSHIP
Chart #12353   Loran: 15233.1 43645.1(4.6) 26598.9

The wreck is located 13 miles southeast of Ocean Beach, in 105 feet of water.

STONE BARGE
Chart #12346   Loran: 26782.1(4) 43728.2

Lying in 48+ feet of water, the unidentified wreck is a popular site for lobstering and spearfishing. It is located about 3 miles off Jones Inlet, New York.

RUMRUNNER - LIZZIE D
Source: AWOIS
Chart #12326   Loran: 26828.9 43696.3
Lat/Long 40/28/18.60 73/39/12.00

The crew of the Lizzie D scuttled their vessel rather than be captured with the "goods" during the days of Prohibition. Lying in 70 to 80 feet of water, divers still recover "spirits" from the almost intact 100-foot tug. Visibility is usually between 15 to 25 feet.

IBERIA
Source: Rick Lippert
Northport, N.Y.
Chart #12263   Loran: 26855.6 43736.2

The freighter Iberia, as with so many other near-shore wrecks, is a twisted mass of decaying metal, serving as home for a wide variety of marine creatures. The scattered wreckage of the 943-ton vessel is popular with divers and fishermen.

On November 10, 1888, the Iberia was off the south shore of Long Island, bound for New York. Near Long Beach, it became enveloped in a dense fog. Travelling from the opposite direction, the liner Umbria did not see the freighter as it crossed its bow. Too late to react, the liner cut through the Iberia's stern section. The old freighter managed to stay afloat for about one day until its bulkheads finally gave way, and it went to the bottom.

The wreckage rests in 60 feet of water, about 4 miles south of Long Beach. Visibility over the site ranges from 5 to 30+ feet.

BLACK WARRIOR
Chart #12326   Loran: 26951.9 43755.2

The sail and steam sidewheel Black Warrior had a rich history before it went aground and sank off Rockaway Inlet, New York, on February 20, 1859. War had nearly been declared over the US mail packet's seizure by the Cubans in 1854. The situation was resolved when that government agreed to return the ship and its cargo. In 1857, a winter storm tore away the vessel's sails and rigging and almost sent the 1,556-ton ship to the bottom. Out of coal, the heavily iced Black Warrior managed to limp back to safety by burning its furniture, bulkheads, and anything else that would keep the boilers going.

In 1859, the Black Warrior laid west of Rockaway Inlet. Over the intervening 125+ years, east-west movement of beach sand, (known as long shore transport), moved the inlet in a westerly direction, leaving the wreck in it present position, a few miles to the east. It lies in about 30 feet of water, a mass of timbers and metal. The shallow wreckage is ideal for novice divers and underwater photographers. Colonies of star coral dot the wreck, with cunner, blackfish, black bass and lobster inhabiting its twisted structure. Visibility is often poor, varying from 5 to 20 feet.

PRINCESS ANNE

Chart #12326 Loran: 43758.0 26968.3

The Old Dominion Line's Princess Anne, left Norfolk, Virginia, on February 3, 1920. Bound for New York, it carried 32 passengers, with a crew of 72 men. From the first day out, the steamer ran into a northeast gale with heavy snow. Three days later, the sea-tossed vessel approached Ambrose Channel, with visibility reduced to nearly zero. Lost, the steamer completely missed the channel buoy and became grounded off Rockaway Point, New York. The passengers and crew were rescued before the Princess Anne began breaking up.

Little of the shallow wreck's structure is left. Visibility at the site is usually poor.

USS TURNER DD 648*

Chart #12326 Loran: 43725.6 26936.4

During World Wars I and II, U-boats sometimes selected targets within a short distance of the coast. On January 3, 1944, the destroyer USS Turner weigh anchor 4 miles off Rockaway Point. The false sense of security that must have been felt by the warship's proximity to land, was suddenly shattered by an enemy torpedo. The initial blast killed most of the ship's officers. Fed by the destroyer's magazines, a second explosion sent the ship to the bottom in 60 feet of water. Survivors were picked up by the Coast Guard cutter, Wanderer.

The badly broken-up wreck rises nearly 30 feet off the bottom. Metal parts taken from the wreck invariably show signs of tremendous blast. The main hazards on the Turner are sharp metal edges and shipping traffic. Visibility on the wreck varies between 5 to 20 feet.

* Edward H. Wiswesser, *Warship Drawings*

116

NEW JERSEY and approaches to NEW YORK

The Atlantic coast of New York and New Jersey has a large number of diveable shipwrecks which are accessible from harbors in both states. Only a fraction of New Jersey's wrecks are covered in this volume; the remainder are a subject perhaps for a future volume.

Just as Rhode Island's shore diving attracts out-of-state divers, so do the New York and New Jersey shipwrecks. Most area dive shops have their own charter boat, or can arrange for one.

Shore diving along New Jersey's coast is often poor due to low visibility. Divers frequent the jetties at Manasquan Inlet, Shark River Inlet, Barnegat Inlet, Brigatine Inlet and other sites. Wrecks such as the Western World (600 feet offshore at Spring Lake) the Pliny (Asbury Park) and the Malta (off Belmar) are reached by small boat or from shore.

WAL-505 AMBROSE RELIEF LIGHTSHIP　　Chart #12326
Loran: 43702.9(3.1) 26912.4(6) ? 43695.7-8 26903.4(6)

It was just before 11 pm on June 23, 1960 that the Central Gulf Steamship Corporation's freighter Green bay prepared to leave Lower New York Bay. Bound for the Red Sea, the ship made its way slowly down Ambrose Channel in heavy rain and fog. Boatswain's Mate, Bobby Pierce, on duty in the Relief Lightship's pilot house, barely had time to sound the general alarm, as the 10,270-ton freighter bore down on the anchored beacon. The Green Bay struck the vessel's starboard side, just behind the mid-section, leaving a 12-foot gash in the lightship's side. Seawater poured into the ship leaving little time for the nine crewmen to escape. Ten minutes after the collision, the Ambrose Relief Lightship sank stern first, in 90 to 100 feet of water.

Lying 8 miles southeast of Rockaway Point and 9 miles east of Sandy Hook, the wreckage rises 20 feet off the bottom. Souvenir hunters will not find much on the well "picked over" wreck. Though the usual variety of area marine life inhabits the wreck, the sometimes very poor visibility makes it difficult to do any photography.

PILOT BOAT - NEW JERSEY
Chart #1232   Loran: 26908.8 43700.9

Built in 1902 at Tottenville, the 148-foot pilot boat New Jersey served New York Harbor. On the morning of July 9, 1914, a dense fog developed along the coastline. The New Jersey had just picked up one of its pilots from the steamer Kelvinbank, when the freighter Manchioneal emerged from the fog and ran into the pilot boat. The 18 men aboard the stricken vessel were rescued by the freighter, moments before it sank to 90 feet below the surface.

The pilot boat rises about 10 feet off a silt bottom. Visibility on and around the wreckage tends to be poor.

MOHAWK - *Coast Guard Vessel*
Chart #12326   Loran: 43670.7(8) 26867.7(8)(2)

The Mohawk was reported to have been rammed and sunk off Sea Bright on October 1, 1917. All aboard were lost. The ship lies in 100+ feet of water, rising to about 66 feet.

PINTA
Chart #12326   Loran: 26880.3(4) 43563.5

The sun had just set on the clear evening of May 7, 1963, when the 194-foot Dutch motorship Pinta collided with British freighter, City of Perth. A distress signal brought out Coast Guard helicopters and 2 cutters to the site, but before help had arrived, the little-damaged, 10,700-ton City of Perth had taken on the ill-fated vessel's crew of 12. Listing to port, the Pinta sank within 48 minutes.

Located 6.5 miles northeast of Asbury Park, New Jersey, the Pinta rests on its port side, in 80+ feet of water. The wreckage has deteriorated somewhat, though it is still mostly intact. The well "picked over" vessel is a shelter for a wide variety of marine fish.

MOHAWK - *Steamship*
Chart #12326   Loran: 43439.9(4.0) 26878.0(7.9)

The Ward Line, operators of the steamship Mohawk, had been plagued with a series of mishaps. The most serious of these was the burning of the Morro Castle on September 8, 1934, with a loss of over 126 lives. The Mohawk was charted in 1934 by the line, to fill in for another of its ships, the Havana, that had run aground·on a Caribbean reef.

On the evening of January 25, 1935, the Mohawk left New York, bound for Cuba. Approximately 6.5 miles off Sea Girt, New

Jersey, the steamship collided with the Norwegian freighter Talisman. Seven years earlier, on May 19, 1929, the Mohawk, then operated by the Clyde Mallory Line, had collided with the steamer Jefferson and grounded itself at Sea Bright. Its second accident was not so lucky. One hour after the mishap, the vessel turned over on its side and sank in almost 80 feet of water. Survivors were picked up by the freighter Limon and the Coast Guard; 46 lives were lost. The Talisman with some damage to its bow, was able to steam on its own to Norfolk, Virginia, for repairs.

The Mohawk sat upright on the bottom, its mast rising 16 feet above the water, until dynamited as a hazard to navigation. The wreckage is located about 7 miles northeast of Shark River Inlet and 1.5 miles south of the Pinta, in 80 feet of water. Divers report that the scattered wreckage is particularly good for lobster.

ARUNDO

Chart #12326   Loran: 43533.9(4.5) 26796.6(8-9)

The 5,163-ton Dutch freighter Arundo was carrying a cargo of trucks bound for Alexandria, Egypt, when it was topedoed by the U-136, on April 28, 1942. The wreckage lies a little over 15 miles off Shark River Inlet, New Jersey, in 125+ feet of water. Divers report plenty of souvenirs on the wreck.

TOLTEN   Source: Sea Grant

Chart #12323   Loran: 26815.3(8) 43360.2(5)

The Tolten was one of five Danish steamers that had been seized by the Chilean government for the duration of World War II. Formerly known as the S.S. Lotta, the 1,858-ton freighter was built in 1938 at Aslborg. In February of 1942, the vessel had discharged a cargo of nitrate at Baltimore and was proceeding to New York in ballast. A U-boat found its mark on March 13, 1942, sending the vessel to the bottom off Barnegat Point, New Jersey. Only one of the 27 crewmen, Julio Faust, survived. He clung to a life raft for almost 12 hours before being picked up by the Coast Guard.

The partially intact ship lies in 90+ feet of water, 13 miles east of Seaside Park, New Jersey.

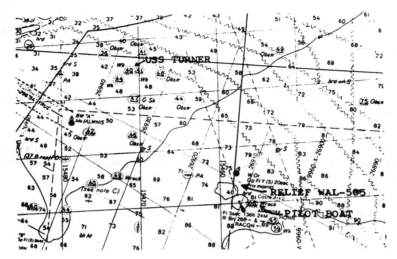

Wrecks: USS Turner, Relief WAL-505, Pilot Boat

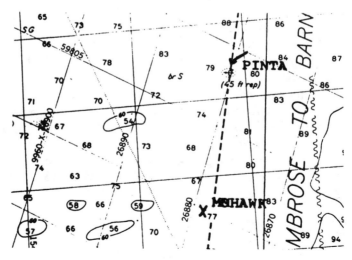

Wrecks: Pinta, Mohawk (steamship)

120

GULFTRADE

Chart #12323   Loran: 26889.0 43263.6(2.9) (bow)

26821.0 43318.2 (stern)

The 6.776-ton American tanker Gulftrade, was only 3.5 miles off Barnegat, New Jersey, when it was torpedoed on March 10, 1942. Just two days earlier, the 5,152-ton Brazilian passenger liner Cayru, had also fallen victim to a U-boat attack. Running without lights in the dark of night, the Gulftrade was sailing from Texas to New York, with a cargo of fuel oil. As the tanker approached Barnegat, it encountered several large vessels. Feeling that there was little danger of attack so close to shore, and fearing a collision even more, Captain Torger Olsen ordered the ship's running lights turned on. It proved to ba a fatal mistake. There was a sudden explosion that tore the 429-foot ship completely in half. Flames leaped from the vessel but were quickly extinguished by a mercifully large wave. Some of the crew took to the three remaining lifeboats while others choose to remain with the stern and were rescued later; 18 were lost and 16 survived.

The bow and stern drifted and went to the bottom almost 11 miles apart! The bow lies 3.5 miles southeast of Barnegat Light, in about 50 feet of water. The stern is located 13 miles northeast of the light, in a depth of 85 feet.

The Loran position of a number of other shipwrecks appear in the appendix.

Inboard Profiles of the USS Bass and San Diego

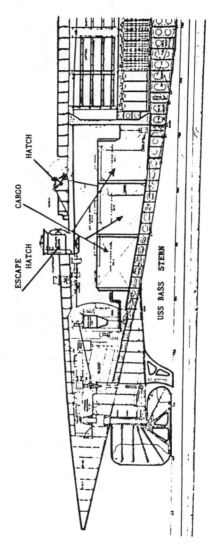

USS BASS: Stern.
National Archives #131536

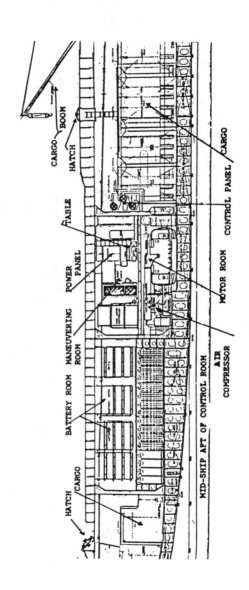

USS BASS: Mid-ship, aft of control room.
National Archives #131536

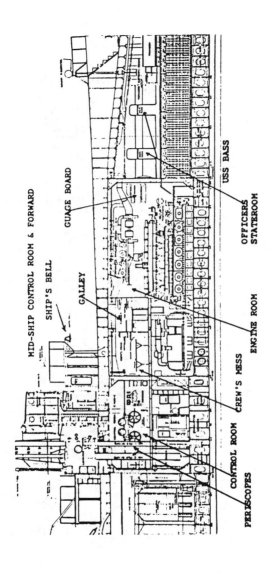

USS BASS: Mid-ship, control room and forward.
National Archives #131536

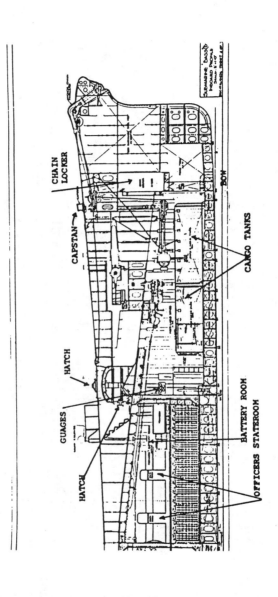

USS BASS: Bow.
National Archives #131536

126

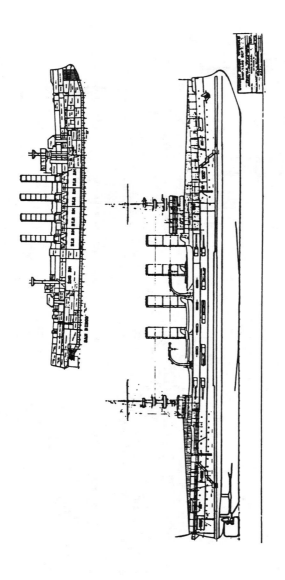

USS SAN DIEGO: Inboard and outboard profiles.
National Archives #11426-E-45

127

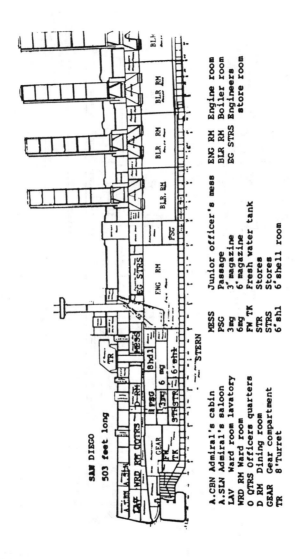

USS SAN DIEGO: Inboard profile. Stern to mid-ship.
National Archives

128

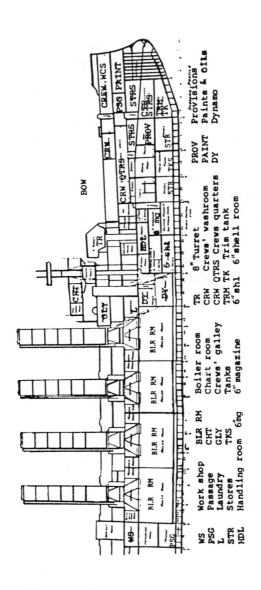

USS SAN DIEGO: Inboard profile. Mid-ship to bow.
National Archives

129

Appendix

The following is a compilation of Loran C and/or Latitude and Longitude positions of wrecks, hangs and obstructions. Sources of the information include divers, trawl fishermen, the National Ocean Service and Sea Grant. From this diver's own experience, about 1 of every 5-6 unknown trawl obstruction (uk obstr), turns out to be a wreck (see Finding a Wreck); the others are rocks, debris or nothing. There is however, the potential of finding an unexplored wreck!

GOOD HUNTING!

Chart #13237 Nantucket Sound and approaches
Chart #13218 Martha's Vineyard to Block Island
Chart #13205 Block Island Sound and approaches
Chart #12353 Shinnecock Light to Fire Island Light
Chart #12326 Fire Island Light to Sea Grit, N.J.
Chart #12323 Sea Grit to Little Egg Inlet
Chart #12318 Little Egg Inlet to Hereford Inlet

	Chart	Lat/Long Loran C	Approx. depth	distance from land point	ID
01	13237	25106.8 43786.4	76+ft	south of Nantucket I.	uk obstr
02	13237	25134.8 43787.3	80 ft	south of Nantucket I.	uk obstr
03	13237	25148.0 43786.1	90+ft	south of Nantucket I.	uk obstr
04	13237	25143.9 43786.1		south of Nantucket I.	uk obstr
05	13237	25164.4 43791.6	87-90	south of Nantucket I.	uk obstr
06	13237	25132.3 43771.6	80-85	south of Nantucket I.	uk obstr
07	13218	25414.2 43868.0	67 ft	1.5 m from Squibnocket Pt	uk obstr
08	13218	25381.8 43827.8	95 ft	6.5 m from Squibnocket Pt	uk obstr
09	13218	25371.7 43822.4	100 ft	7.5 m from Squibnocket Pt	uk obstr
10	13218	25376.9 43814.8	103 ft	8.5 m SE of Squibnocket Pt	uk obstr
11	13218	25368.5 43807.1	110+ ft	9.5 m from Squibnocket Pt	uk obstr
12	13218	25352.1 43801.7	120 ft	10.5 miles of Squibnocket Pt	uk obstr

	Chart	Lat/Long Loran C	Approx. depth	distance from land point	ID
13	13218	25339.7 43785.7	140 ft	13.0 m from Squibnocket Pt	uk obstr
14	13218	25413.4 43800.5	116 ft	10.5 m from Squibnocket Pt	uk obstr
15	13218	25420.4 43792.6	115 ft	11.5 m from Squibnocket Pt	uk obstr
16	13218	25408.4 43796.0	130 ft	11 m from Squibnocket Pt	uk obstr
17	13218	25534.5 43963.9	54 ft	Buzzard's Bay	uk obstr
18	13218	25512.9 43838.6	115 ft	12 m SW of Squibnocket Pt	uk obstr
19	13218	25569.2 43844.1	111 ft	14.5 m SW of Squibnocket Pt	uk obstr
20	13218	25503.4 43820.5	100 ft	14.5 m SW of Squibnocket Pt	uk obstr
21	13218	25531.5 43793.8	116 ft	17.5 m SW of Squibnocket Pt	uk obstr
22	13218	25530.4 43896.6	100+ft	5.5 m W of Gay Head	uk obstr
23	13218	41/22/15 71/23/18.60	85 ft	off Newport	Doris
24	13218	41/19/46.64 (bow) 71/25/46.97 41/19/33.05 (stern — see text) 71/25/47.48		off Point Judith, RI	Black Point
25	13205	43945.9 14525.7	80+ft	West of Point Judith	Heroine
26	13205	25985.4 43912.1	97 ft	8 m south Watch Hill	wreck?
27	13205	26004.0 43950.8	120 to 74 ft	3 m south Watch Hill	wreck? (see #28)
28	13205	25998.1 43949.0	120 ft	3 + m south Watch Hill	Larchmont
29	13214	41/16/26.5 72/02/38.8	40 ft	NW of Fishers I.	pos wreck
30	13205	25917.84 43937.24	125 ft	North of Block I.	Amelia M Periera
31	13205	25900.1 43923.3	109 ft	4.5 m north Block I.	uk obstr
32	13205	41/07/12.0 71/34/12	70+ft	SW of Block I.	Pocahontas Schooner
33	13205	41/08/54 71/36/48		Off Block I	Edward Luckenback

	Chart	Lat/Long Loran C	Approx. depth	distance from land point	ID
34	13205	41/13/54 71/34/42		off Sandy Pt Block I	Princess Agusta
35	13205	43820.7 25799.1	150 ft	South of Block I.	Acid Barge
36	13205	14540.0 43836.5	85 ft	4.5 m south Block I.	Apple Tree wreck
37	13205	25809.1 43854.7	83 ft	13 m. south Block I.	uk obstr
38	13205	25891.9 43791.3	163 ft	13.5 m SW Block I.	uk obstr
39	13205	25906.5 43828.9	130 ft	8 m east of Montauk	uk obstr
40	13205	25952.54 43842.99	60+ft	Montauk Shoal	Snug Harbor
41	13205	25937.9 43804.9	142 ft	8.5 m south Montauk	uk obstr
42	12353	26241.3 43774.6	97ft	4.5 m off Southampton	uk obstr
43	12353	26220.6 43776.3	100 ft	4.5 m off Southampton	uk obstr
44	12353	26190.0 43782.4	103 ft	5 m off Southampton	uk obstr
45	12353	26217.0 43769.3	110 ft	5.5 m off Southampton	uk obstr
46	12353	26213.9 43769.3	110 ft	6 m off Southampton	uk obstr
47	12353	26183.7 43768.4	119 ft	6.5 m off Southampton	uk obstr
48	12353	26214.4 43755.5	116 to 132ft	7 m off Southampton	uk obstr
49	12353	26199.7 43766.5	115 ft	6.5 m off Southampton	uk obstr
50	12353	26175.1 43751.3	125+ft	7 m off Southampton	uk obstr
51	12353	26195.6 43743.7	138 ft	8 m off Southampton	uk obstr
52	12353	26193.9 43740.3	136 ft	8.5 m off Southampton	uk obstr
53	12353	26183.5 43733.0	139+ft	9.5 m off Southampton	uk obstr
54	12353	26180.9 43716.4	145 ft	13 m off Southampton	uk obstr
55	12353	26172.9 43714.2	148 ft	13 m off Southampton	uk obstr

	Chart	Lat/Long Loran C	Approx. depth	distance from land point	ID
56	12353	26204.0(3-6)180+ 43576.2(3-6) ft		28 m off Southampton	Coimbra war loss
57	12353	26302.7 43765.1	90+ft	5 m off Shinnecock	uk obstr
58	12353	26310.8 43715.0	120- 122 ft	12 m off Shinnecock	uk obstr
59	12353	26307.2 43707.0	115- 130?ft	13 miles off Shinnecock	uk obstr
60	12353	26296.6 43692.9	135+ft	14.5 m. off Shinnecock	uk obstr
61	12353	26499.6 43767.5	75 feet	1 mile off Great S Beach	uk obstr
62	12353	26484.2 43725.2	100 ft	5.5 miles off Great S Beach	uk obstr
63	12353	26497.3 43692.4	96 feet	9 miles off Great S Beach	uk obstr
64	12353	26447.8 43689.5	126- 130 ft	11.5 m off Great S Beach	uk obstr
65	12353	26449.2 43683.1	120- 125 ft	12 miles off Great S Beach	uk near Oregon
66	12353	26478.1 43671.8	120 ft	12 miles off Great S Beach	uk obstr
67	12353	26452.7(2,9) 43676.3(7) 125ft		13 miles off Great S Beach	wreck of Oregon
68	12353	26451.8 43567.1	121 ft	13+m south of Great S Beach	uk obstr
69	12353	26481.8 43653.9	130 ft	13.5 m off Great S Beach	uk obstr
70	12353	26472.3 43653.4	135 ft	13.5 m off Great S Beach	uk obstr
71	12353	26605.9 43716.8	75 ft	4.5 miles off Ocean Beach	airplane
72	12353	26609.4-6(9) 43610.2(5) 87 ft		8.4 m off Ocean Beach	Skippy - gunboat
73	12353	26566.4 43621.6	113 ft	15 m off Ocean Beach	uk obstr
74	12353	26617.3 43665.7	95 ft	10.5 m off Saltaire	uk obstr
75	12353	26587.4 43659.6	105 ft	11.5 m off Saltaire	wreck
76	12353	26598.9 43644.9 15233.1	105 ft	12 miles off Saltaire	Fire Is. lightship
77	12353	26592.7 43644.4	109 ft	12 miles off Saltaire	uk obstr

134

	Chart	Lat/Long Loran C	Approx. depth	distance from land point	ID
78	12326	26559.9 43741.2	45 feet	2 miles off Fire Island	uk obstr
79	12353	26643.3 43707.5	80 feet	4.5 miles off Fire Island	uk obstr
80	12326	26618.9 43704.7	81 feet	4.5 miles off Fire Island	uk obstr
81	12353	26529.5 43712.8	85 feet	6 miles off Fire Island	uk near Wolcott
82	12353	26518.1(6) 43712.8 15146.8	84 ft	6 miles off Fire Island	schooner Wolcott
83	12353	26516.3 43700.3	88 ft	7.5 m off Fire Island	uk obstr
84	12353	26527.9 43647.8	113 ft	13.5 m off Fire Island	uk obstr
85	12326	26601.1 43591.3	123 ft	17.5 m off Fire Island	uk near Yankee
86	12316	26609.3(4) 43592.1(4)	120 ft	17.5 m off Fire Island	wreck of Yankee
87	12326	26607.2 43590.4	120 ft	17.5 m off Fire Island	wreck?
88	12326	26606.2 43589.0(2)	115 ft	17.5 m off Fire Island	wreck
89	12326	26662.5 43695.1	80 feet	6.5 m off Fire Is Inlet	bad hang
90	12326	26665.1 43610.3	110 ft	15.5 m off Fire Is Inlet	uk obstr
91	12326	26673.1 43574.6	110 ft	20.5 m off Fire Is Inlet	uk obstr
92	12326	26671.5 43567.5	113 ft	21 m off Fire Is Inlet	uk obstr
93	12326	26669.2 43555.8	119 ft	22 m off Fire Is Inlet	uk obstr
94	12326	26626.9 43514.8	128 ft	26 m off Fire Is Inlet	uk obstr
95	12326	26698.2 43682.4	70 ft	9 miles off Cedar Is Beach	uk obstr
96	12326	26703.6 43664.8	75-80 feet	10 m off Jones Beach	uk obstr
97	12326	26757.6 43661.8	83 feet	10+ m off Jones Beach	uk obstr
98	12326	26791.4(6) 43642.2(1)	70 feet	9+ miles off Jones Inlet	Three Sisters
99	12326	26912.5 43702.8(9)	81 ft	Ambrose Light	wreck

Chart	Lat/Long Loran C	Approx. depth	distance from land point	ID
100 12326	26863.8 43580.9	149 ft	11 m off Elberon,NJ	oil wreck
101 12326	26840.0 43547.3	160 ft	11 m off Asbury Pk	oil wreck
102 12326	26810.9 43562.3	95 ft	13.5 m off Asbury Pk	uk obstr
103 12326	26832.0 43549.4(6)	140+ft	12+ m off Asbury Pk	Choapa
104 12326	26868.5 43527.4	88 ft	off Belmar	Ranger?
105 12326	26796.6 43533.9(4.6)	116 ft	14 m off Skark R. Inlet	Arundo
106 12326	26889.0 43528.9	75 ft	6 m off Belmar,NJ	wreck?
107 12323	26910.2 43499.3	50 ft	off Sea Girt	Reef Barge
108 12323	26907.9 43447.8	72 ft	3.5 m off Mantoloking	Glory?
109 12323	26905.9 43444.8	74 ft	4 m off Mantoloking	wreck
110 12323	26594.1 43659.1	65 ft	off Mantoloking	wreck
111 12323	26911.0 43415.9	68 ft	3 m off Lavallette	uk obstr
112 12323	26884.4 43408.1	69 ft	5.5+ m off Lavallette	wreck
113 12323	26844.1 43417.6	84 ft	10+ m east Lavallette	uk obstr
114 12323	26815.3(8) 43360.5(1)	92 ft 51	off Seaside Pk	wreck of Tolten
115 12323	26917.2 43361.2	60 ft	2.5 m south Seaside Pk	uk obstr
116 12323	26899.2 43368.7	60 ft	4 m south Seaside Pk	uk obstr
117 12323	26890.4 43355.6	62 ft	5 m south Seaside Pk	wreck?
118 12323	26878.7 43439.8	67 ft	8.5 m NE Barnegat Inlet	uk obstr
119 12323	26822.6 43320.8	80 ft	12.4 m NE Barnegat Inlet	uk obstr·
120 12323	26862.2 43308.8	78 ft	8 m E Barnegat Inlet	wreck?
121 12323	26908.1 43303.6	47 ft	3 m NE Barnegat Inlet	uk obstr

Chart	Lat/Long Loran C	Approx. depth	distance from land point	ID
122 12323	26889.2 43298.8	63 ft	4.5 m NE Barnegat Inlet	uk obstr
123 12323	26895.7 43289.5	52 ft	2.5 m NE Barnegat Inlet	wreck?
124 12323	26856.1 43297.9	76 ft	8 m E Barnegat Inlet	wreck?
125 12323	26829.6 43291.6	82 ft	10.5.m E of Barnegat Inlet	uk obstr
126 12323	26877.0 43270.7	70 ft	4.5 m E Barnegat Inlet	uk obstr
127 12323	26846.8 43276.5	80 ft	8 m E Barnegat Inlet	uk obstr
128 12323	26777.2 43288.9	85+ft	16 m E Barnegat Inlet	uk obstr
129 12323	26899.1 43248.2	49 ft	3.5 m S Barnegat Inlet	uk obstr
130 12323	26876.6 43244.5	69 ft	5 m S Barnegat Inlet	wreck
131 12323	26854.7 43242.2	76+ft	8 m SE Loveladies	uk obstr
132 12323	26850.3 43241.4	76+ft	8.5 m SE Loveladies	uk obstr
133 12323	26804.1 43243.3	97 ft	12.5 m S Barnegat Inlet	uk obstr
134 12323	26802.7 43237.3	96 ft	12.5 m S Barnegat Inlet	uk obstr
135 12323	26787.7 43229.8	60 ft	14.5 m S Barnegat Inlet	uk obstr
136 12323	26876.3 43234.8	67 ft	5.5 m SE Barnaget Inlet	uk obstr
137 12323	26889.2 43225.5	56 ft	6.5 m NE Ship Bottom	uk obstr
138 12323	26910.9 43223.7	39 ft	2 m E Harvey Cedars	uk obstr
139 12323	26890.2 43211.7	65 ft	6 m NE Ship Bottom	wreck?
140 12323	26876.2 43212.9	70+ft	7.5 m NE Ship Bottom	uk obstr
141 12323	26867.8 43208.0	74 ft	8.5 m NE Ship Bottom	uk obstr
142 12323	26850.6 43223.2	77 ft	8 m S Barnegat Inlet	uk obstr
143 12323	26887.2 43199.4	60+ft	6 m E Ship Bottom	uk obstr

Chart	Lat/Long Loran C	Approx. depth	distance from land point	ID
144 12323	26848.1 43215.3	79 ft	11 m E Ship Bottom	wreck?
145 12323	26870.1 43200.1	72 ft	8 m SE Ship Bottom	uk obstr
146 12323	26864.8 43201.6	76 ft	8.5 m NE Ship Bottom	uk obstr
147 12323	26837.6 43202.8	83 ft	12 m SE Ship Bottom	uk obstr
148 12323	26832.7 43192.0	85 ft	12 m SE Ship Bottom	uk obstr
149 12323	26801.2 43200.2	92+ft	15.5 m E Ship Bottom	uk obstr
150 12323	26788.0 43196.1	80 ft	17 m E Ship Bottom	uk obstr
151 12323	26804.3 43193.0	95- 100 ft	15.5 m SE Barnegat Inlet	uk obstr
152 12323	26686.8 43190.3	100 ft	16 m E Ship Bottom	uk obstr
153 12323	26857.7 43181.2	78 ft	9.2 m SE Ship Bottom	uk obstr
154 12323	26841.0 43178.3	86 ft	8 m SE Ship Bottom	uk obstr
155 12323	26911.9 43166.4	54 ft	4 m SE Ship Bottom	uk obstr
156 12323	26901.4 43159.8	63 ft	6 m SE Ship Bottom	uk obstr
157 12323	26894.4 43154.1	58 ft	6 m SE Ship Bottom	uk obstr
158 12323	26876.9 43148.8	74 ft	8 m SE Ship Bottom	uk obstr
159 12323	26870.8 43146.8	80 ft	8.5 m SE Ship Bottom	uk obstr
160 12323	26868.1 43150.4	78 ft	10 m SE Beach Haven	uk obstr
161 12323	28851.4 43151.5	81 ft	11.5 m E Beach Haven	uk obstr
162 12323	26908.0 43133.9	56 ft	7 m NE Little Egg Inlet	uk obstr
163 12323	26892.8 43136.2	57 ft	10 m NE Little Egg Inlet	uk obstr
164 12323	26834.2 43125.8	76 ft	13 m SE Beach Haven Crest	uk obstr
165 12323	26805.5 43119.1	87 ft	19+m Little Egg Hbr	wreck

Chart	Lat/Long Loran C	Approx. depth	distance from land point	ID
166 12318	26921.0 43105.2	56 ft	4 m off Little Egg Inlet	uk obstr
167 12318	26921.2 43110.3	58 ft	5 m S Little Egg Inlet	uk obstr
168 12318	26814.4 42956.7	92 ft	26 m E Great Egg Hbr	wreck
169 12318	26896.5 42944.5	84 ft	Fish Haven (see chart)	schooner America
170 12318	26895.4 42944.0	84 ft	Fish Haven (see chart)	Pauline Marie
171 12318	26897.3 42943.3	84 ft	Fish Haven (see chart)	First Lady
172 12318	26896.1 42948.1	84 ft+-	Fish Haven (see chart)	Marana Abaco
173 13003	26856.8 43474.8		offshore	wreck
174 13003	25355.0 43736.0		offshore	wreck
175 13003	25249.8 43694.7		offshore	wreck
176 13003	25406.8 43764.2		offshore	airplane
177 13003	25405.9 43767.0		offshore	airplane
178 13003	25499.1 43706.5		offshore	airplane
179 13003	25478.5 43712.9		offshore	wreck
180 13003	25469.2 43735.6		offshore	airplane
181 13003	25854.1 43313.1		offshore	wreck
182 13003	26663.0 42604.9		offshore	wreck
183 13003	26765.2 42134.8		offshore	wreck

UNC Sea Grant would like to hear what you found at these sites, along with your own unit's Loran C numbers. UNC Sea Grant, Marine Advisory Service, PO Box 699, Manteo, N.C. 27954

SUGGESTED READING

LORAN C

Block, Richard A. 1982. Fundamentals of Loran C. Houma, La.: Marine Education Textbooks

USCG 1980. Loran C User Handbook, COMDTINST M16562.3 Washington, DC: U.S. Government Printing Office (A well written manual)

MARINE ANIMALS

Arnold, Augusta F. 1968. The Sea Beach at Ebb-tide. New York: Dover

Gosner, Kenneth L. 1971. Guide to the Identification of Marine and Estuarine Invertebrates. New York: Wiley (This book is for professionals; difficult to use)

Gosner, K.L. 1979. A Field Guide to the Atlantic Seashore. Houghton Mifflin Co., Boston, Ma. (An excellent guide)

Meinkoth, Norman A. 1981. The Audubon Society Field Guide to North American Seashore Creatures. New York: Knopf (Uses color photographs)

Miner, Roy Waldo 1950. Field Book to Seashore Life. New York: Putnam

Smith, Ralph I., ed. 1964. Keys to Marine Invertebrates of the Woods Hole Region. Woods Hole, Ma: Marine Biological Laboratory

Zinn, J. Donald 1975. The Handbook for Beach Strollers from Maine to Cape Hatteras. Chester, Ct.: Pequot Press

MARINE FISH

Bigelow, Henry B. and Schroeder, William C. 1964. Fishes of the Gulf of Maine. Washington, DC: U.S. Government Printing Office (A classic - excellent)

Breder, Charles M. 1948. Field Book of Marine Fishes of the Atlantic Coast. New York: Putnam

Thomson, Keith S., Weed, W.H. and Taruski, A.G. 1971. Saltwater Fishes of Connecticut, Bull #105. Distributed by the State Library, Hartford, Ct. (Well illustrated)

SHIPWRECKS

Berman, Bruce D. 1972. Encyclopedia of American Shipwrecks. Boston: Mariners Press (A good start for any wreck researcher)

Carter, Margaret M. 1973. Shipwrecks on the Shores of Westerly. (A historical account, self published)

Hocking, Charles 1969. Dictionary of Disasters at Sea During the Age of Steam, 1824-1962. London: Lloyds Register of Shipping.

Jenny, Jim 1980. In Search of Shipwrecks. Cranbury, N.J.: A.S. Barnes (Unfortunately, the author did not give the exact location (Loran) of the wrecks)

Krotee, Walter and Krotee, Richard 1968. Shipwrecks off the New Jersey Coast. Philadelphia: Underwater Society of America (A good local resource)

Lonsdale, Adrian L. and Kaplan, H.R. 1964. A Guide to Sunken Ships in American Waters. Arlington, Va.: Compass Publ. (A good research tool)

National Ocean Service (NOS) 1983. Automated Wreck and Obstruction Information System (AWOIS) (National Ocean Service,

Distribution, N/CG33, Riverdale, Md. 20737) (Most of the positions given in Lat/Long.)

Northeast Advisory Council 1982. A Sportdiver's Handbook for Historic Shipwrecks: Tools and Techniques. Sea Grant Publ. (Northeast Marine Advisory Council, 15 Garrison Ave., Durham, N.H. 03824)

McGee, James A. and Tillett, R. Hughes 1983. Hangs and Obstructions. Univ. N.C. Sea Grant Publ UNC SG-83-01 (Marine Resources Ctr., PO Box 699, Manteo, N.C. 27954) (Some of the Loran C positions are conversions from Loran A, thus subject to some inaccuracy)

O'Keefe, M. Timothy, ed. 1975. International Divers Guide. Underwater Society of America

Quinn, W.P. 1979. Shipwrecks Around New England. Orleans, Ma.: Lower Cap Publ. (photographs and text)

Rattray, J.E. 1955. Ships Ashore. New York: Coward, McCann (Historical accounts)

Rattray, J.E. 1973. The Perils of the Port of New York. New York: Dodd, Mead & Co. (Very helpful)

TIDES AND CURRENTS

White, R.E. Eldridge Tide and Pilot Book, Boston, Ma: R.E. White Publ. (Updated yearly)

UNDERWATER PHOTOGRAPHY

Strykowski, Joe 1974. Divers and Cameras. Northfield, Il: Dacor Corp.

OTHER RESOURCES

National Archives, Washington D.C. 20408 (photographs of warships and ship's plans prior to WW II)

Warship Drawings, Edward H. Wiswesser, 407 North 25th St., Pennside, Reading, Pa. 19606

INDEX

Accidents, 151
American eel, 14
Anchor Beach, CT, 60
Anemone(s), 24, **28**
Arches, RI, 92
Ascent line, 21
Bartlett's Reef, 2, **71**
Bay scallop, 25, **27**
Bayville, NY, 37
Beavertail Pt., RI, 87
Bends, 151
Black sea bass, **19**
Backfish, 17
Block Island, **93**, 94
Bridgeport, CT, 54
Butterfish, 9, **19**
Cable & Anchor Reef, 45
Castle Hill, RI, 90
Clay Pt., NY, 77
Clinton, CT, 70
Cockenoe Is., CT, 48
Cold Spring Hbr., NY, 39
Comb jelly, 9, **10**, 25
Conanicut Is., RI, 87, 89
Conger eel, 14
Coral(s), 25
Crab(s), 7, 8, **27**, 31
Crane Neck Pt., NY, **49**, 55
Cunner, 17
Current(s), 3, 4
DAN, 151

Depth, 3
Duck Is., CT, **65**, 70
Duck Pond, NY, 66
Eatons Neck, NY, **44**, 47
Eelpout, 14
Enders Is., CT, 80
Execution Rks., **33**, 34, 36
Falkner Is., CT, 63
Fan worm, **29**, 31
Fishers Is, NY, **75**, 76
Fish, see specific variety
Flounder, **18**, 19, **29**
Fort Getty, RI, 87
Fort Wetherill, RI, **83**, 89
Gooseberry Is., RI, 92
Goosefish, 16
Great Capt. Is., CT, 38
Green Bridge, RI, 91
Greens Ledge, CT, **41**, 42
Greenport, NY, 67
Greenwich Pt., CT, 39, **41**
Grubby, 15
Guilford, CT, 63
Gulf Stream, 1
Hake, 16
Hammonasset, CT, 69
Harkness Pk., CT, 70, **71**
Hope Is., RI, 89
Horton Pt., NY, **65**, 66
Hydroid, 24, **28**
Inlet Pt., NY, 67
Jamestown, RI, 87

Jellyfish, 9, **10**, 25, **26**
Jennings Pt., NY, 108, **110**
King's Beach, RI, 91
Land's End, RI 92
Latimer Reef Light, 78
Ling, 16
Lloyd Neck, NY, 39
Lobster, 6, 31
Long Island, south shore, 108
Long Island Sound, 34
Loran C, 20
Madison, CT, 69
Mantis shrimp, **30**, 31
Matinecock, Pt., **33**, 35, 36
Mattituck Inlet, **61**, 66
Mola mola, 19
Montauk, NY, 109, **110**
Mount Misery Shl., 57, **58**
Mount Sinai, NY, 62
Narragansett, RI, 86
Narragansett Bay, 89
New Haven, CT, **58**, 62
New London, CT, 73, 74, 76
New London Ledge, 74
New Jersey, 115
Newport, RI, **88**, 90
North Dumpling, NY, 78
North Hill, NY, 76
Northern puffer, **19**
Nudibranch, 25, **26**
Ocean Beach, CT, 74
Ocean sunfish, 19
Octopus, 1
Old Field Pt., NY, 57
Oyster toadfish, 9, **30**
Parsonage Pt., NY, 37
Pecks Ledge Light, CT, 47

Penetration line, 21
Penfield Reff, CT, **44**, 54
Permits, 8
Phytoplankton, 4
Pinnacle, RI, 95
Pipefish, 15
Pirate Cove, RI, 91
Pleasure Beach, CT, 70
Point Judith, RI **83**, 84
Porgy, (scup), **19**
Race Rock, NY, 3, 77
Ram Is., CT., 80
Ray(s), 11, 12
Reeves Beach, NY, 64
Rhode Island, 81
Riverhead, NY, 64
Roanoke, Pt., NY, 64
Rock eel, 14
Sandlaunce, 15, 46
Scallop, 25, **27**
Sea Cliff, NY, 36
Sea horse, 32
Sea rave, 16
Sea stars, 31
Seaside Regional Center, CT,
    70
Shark(s), 11, **12**, **13**
Sheffield Is., CT, 50
Sherwood Is., CT, 50
SHIPWRECKS:
    Acid barge, 133
    Airplane, 64, 114, 139
    Ambrose Lightship, 117,
        120
    Amelia M. Periera, 132
    America, 139
    Andrea Doria, 103, **104**

146

Apple Tree wreck, 98
Artificial reef, **49**, 55
Arundo, 119
At Ease, 43
Atlantic, steamer, 76
Barataria, tug, 67
Barges, Reeves Beach, 64
Bass, sub, 98, **99**, **123**, **124**, **125**, **126**
Black Diamond, 96
Black Point, 85, 132
Black Warrior, 115
Blue Hummer, 39
Cabin criuser, 62
Cape Race, barge, 43
Capitol City, 37
Captain Lawrence, 87
Celtic, tug, 43
Choapa, 135
Coal barge, 36
Coimbra, 105
Columbia, 78
Condor, 40
Defense, 3, **71**, 73
Dodger, 114
Doris, 132
Dredging barge, 38
Duck Pond wreck, 66
Edward Luckenback, 132
Essex, 95
First Lady, 139
Fishing boat, 37
G-2, 72
George Hudson, 81
Glen Island, **33**, 35, **50**
Glory, 136
Grecian, 98, **99**

Gulf Trade, **101**, 121
Gwendoline Steers, tug, 46
Hercules, tug, 83
Heroine, 84
Hope Is. wreck, 89
Hussar, 2
Hylton Castle, 112, **113**
Iberia, 115
Isabel, 39
J-24, 40
John A. Downs, tug, 69
Karen-E, 68
L-8, 86
Larchmont, 3, **52**, 82
Lazy Days, 76
Lexington, **52**, 56
Lightburne, **93**, 94
Lightship, 114
Llewellyn Holland, 92
Lydia Skolfield, 90
Mackin's Wreck, 42, **50**
Maine, **33**, 34
Malamton, 95
Marana Abaco, 139
Mohawk, RC, 118
Mohawk, steamer, 118, **120**
Montana, **92**, 95
Noyack Bay Wreck, 109
Ohio, USS, 108
Oil wreck (s), 135
Old Scow, 45
Olinda, 77
Onondaga, 3, **53**, **79**, 81
Onward, 78
Oregon, **100**, 109

147

Panther, tug, 109
Pauline Marie, 139
Pilot Boat, 118, **120**
Pinta, 118, **120**
Pocahontas, 132
Poling Bros., East, 38
Poling Bros., West, 37
Princess Agusta, 133
Princess Anne, 116
Ranger, 136
Reef barge, 136
Resor, RP, 107
Rhode Island, **52**, 85
Rumrunner, **113**, 115
Rye Cliff, 36
Sailboat, 18-foot, 36
Sailboat, 21-foot, 36
San Diego, **100**, 112,
   113, 127, 128, 129
Skippy, gunboat, 134
Small barge, 50
Snug Harbor, 108
S.E. Spring, 38
Steel barge, 69, 74
Stolt Dagali, 107
Stone barge, 114
Sub at Bayville, 37
Sugar boat, 38
Tennyson, 109
Texas Tower, 106
Thames (Sugar boat), 38
Thames, tug, 68
Thelma-Phoebe, **75**, 78
Thomas Tomlinson, 48
Three Sisters, 135
Tolten, 119
Traveler, schooner, 63

Turner, **101**, 116, **120**
Two Brothers, **93**, 96
U-853, **93**, 96
Unknown wreck(s), 36,
   50, 56, 69, 77, 85
Vanderbilt, 35, 77
Varanger, 105
Wolcott, 111
Wooden drydock, 63
Yankee, 135
Skate(s), 11, **13**
Smithtown Bay, 47, **49**, 54
Southhold, NY, 66
Sponge, 11, 24
Stamford, CT, 39
State Pier #5, RI, 86
Stonington, CT, **79**, 80
Stratford, CT, **58**, 60
Stratford Shoal, **49**, 59
Striped bass, 18
Summer flounder, **18**, 19
Target Rock NY, 46
Tautog, (blackfish),17
Tether line, 4, 21
Threadfin, 17
Tide(s), 2
Toadfish, 9, **30**
Tomcod, 17
Tube worm, **29**, 31
Underwater photography, 22
Visibility,4
Wading River, NY, 62
Watch Hill, RI, **79**, 82
Water, 4, 5
Waterford, CT, 70
Wicopessett Psg, NY, 77
Windowpane flounder, **18**

Winter flounder, 19, **29**
Woodmont, CT, 60
Wreck(s), see
  SHIPWRECKS
Wreck symbols, 21

DIVING ACCIDENTS
Signs and symptoms

BENDS

unusual fatigue, dizziness
itching, skin rash
pain in arms and legs
numbness, staggering,
paralysis
shortness of breath
violent cough
loss of conciousness

AIR EMBOLISM

dizziness, blurred vision
pain in chest
bloody froth from nose
    or mouth
disorientation
personality changes
numbness, tingling
paralysis, convulsions
loss of conciousness,
no breathing, death

Skip breathing, overexertion or equipment malfunctions can cause carbon dioxide build-up, leading to difficulty in breathing, headache, dizziness, nausea, confusion, muscle twitching and/or loss of conciousness.

Symptoms can arise immediately, to about 24 hours after a dive. *Emergency procedure* : Lay the victim down with the left side down, and the head low. Administer oxygen. Even if the symptoms subside rapidly after administrating oxygen, consult a physician.

NATIONAL DIVING ACCIDENT NETWORK (919) 684-8111
Source: Mebane, G.Y., Dick, A.P., 1982. DAN Manual. Durham, Duke Univ.

SAFETY AFLOAT: U.S. COAST GUARD

The vigilant eyes and ears of the U.S. Coast Guard have rescued many a mariner in distress. The service monitors VHF, channel 16 and in some cases CB, channel 9. Shoreline communities have marine police departments and Auxillary Coast Guard units that also monitor VHF and sometimes CB. CB, however, tends to be crowded even on the emergency channel 9, and its range is often poor, thus, it is best to use VHF.